Praise

'If leadership is measured in moments, this book shows you how to make those moments matter. The Shiftcode Model is both simple and profound, giving leaders a reliable compass for uncertain times. Preetie Boler's insights will help you shift from reactivity to intentionality with lasting impact.'
  — **Emeritus Professor Gary Martin FAIM**,
      CEO, Australian Institute of Management
      Western Australia

'What I love about this book is that it doesn't just talk about leadership – it makes you reflect on your own behaviours and gives you practical steps to shift them. The practices have already helped me strengthen my effectiveness as a leader.'
  — **John Pirie**, Head of FM, Western Australia
      and Resources, Programmed by Persol

'One of the most valuable takeaways for me was reframing leadership from "control" to "influence." This simple yet powerful shift creates more flexibility and resilience in how leaders navigate complex situations. The book doesn't just challenge old paradigms – it equips leaders with the mindset and tools to thrive in today's dynamic workplace.'
  — **Rob Thomson**, General Manager,
      Government Sector, Programmed Facility
      Management

'If leadership is measured in moments, this book shows you how to make those moments matter.'

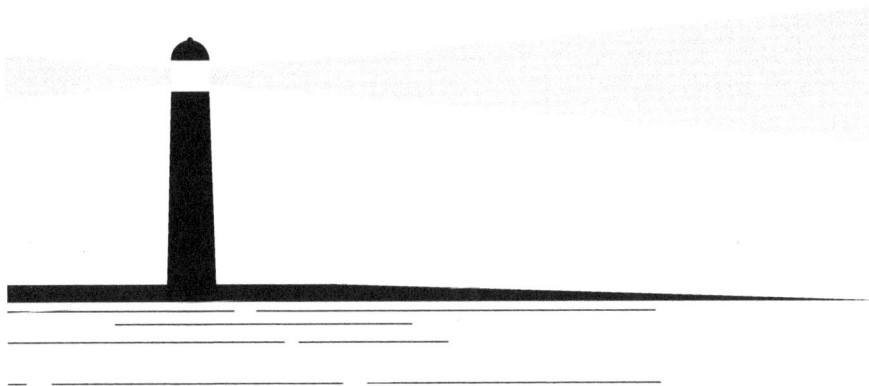

Shiftcode Leadership

A guide to building thriving teams and a positive workplace culture

Preetie Boler

R^ethink

First published in Great Britain in 2025
by Rethink Press (www.rethinkpress.com)

Speech bubble icon © agus raharjo
Sailboat icon © Nanik haq
Lighthouse icon © Siipkan Creative
Anchor icon © Bernd Lakenbrink
Waves icon © Ishaq_hmad

Disclaimer

The case studies, examples, and stories in this book are inspired by experiences, personal and shared from leadership, workplaces, and coaching contexts. To protect the privacy of individuals and organisations, identifying details such as names, roles, locations, and circumstances have been changed. In some instances, scenarios have been blended or presented as composite and illustrative examples. The purpose of these stories is not to recount events exactly as they occurred, but to illustrate the behavioural patterns, challenges, and insights that leaders can learn from. The lessons remain authentic, even where the details have been altered.

Contents

Preface

I didn't write this book because I had it all figured out. I wrote it because I had to figure out how to survive and then how to lead, live, and rise.

It was 18 September 2006, and I was lying on the cold tiles of my bathroom floor, broken in every way a woman can be broken. I was a lawyer, a wife, and a mother, but at that time, I didn't feel like any of those things. My marriage had quietly collapsed, my son clung to his nanny more than to me, and beneath my mask of competence and control, I was drowning.

I wasn't thinking about leadership then but about how to make the pain stop. Six hours into the silence, something inside me stirred. Not strength or clarity.

Just a flicker of will. I stood up, walked to my desk, picked up a pen, and wrote.

I wrote eighteen pages of raw truth. No filters or performance, just pain. A contract with my future self. That journal became my lifeline and, unknowingly, the beginning of my transformation.

Over the years, I've learned that personal breakdowns don't stay personal. They follow you and seep into how you show up at work, how you lead, how you speak, and how you behave under pressure.

I thought I'd compartmentalised my pain. I buried myself in work and became the problem-solver in the storm. As a senior legal counsel in the construction industry, I was the one who held everything together when major multimillion-dollar disputes spiralled. All that unprocessed emotion, though – like shame and guilt – together with the relentless pressure to prove I was enough, leaked into my leadership.

Until one day, it erupted.

A high-stakes negotiation was falling apart. The room was tense, voices were raised, and everyone was posturing to protect their turf. I tried to stay calm, but something cracked. I slammed my hand on the table and snapped, 'Enough!'

The room fell silent, but not the kind of silence that brings resolution. It was the kind that deepens disconnection, and that moment magnified the conflict.

That night, as I sat alone, with an ice pack on my hand and shame rising in my chest, the truth hit hard: I had replicated the behaviours I once swore I'd never mirror. My tone had shut people down, my need for control had eroded trust, and my reactivity had sabotaged collaboration. It wasn't just their behaviour that was the problem. It was mine, too.

That was my turning point.

For the first time, I saw clearly that leadership excellence isn't about what you know but about how you show up, especially when things don't go to plan. That moment became the seed that grew into everything I teach now, which evolved not from a theory but from a lived truth. I wondered: what if leadership isn't about fixing the chaos around you but about shifting the behaviour within you?

That question stayed with me.

Once I started seeing leadership as a behavioural practice, not just a professional role, I couldn't unsee it. Over three decades working across legal, construction, and corporate environments, I witnessed how behaviour, not capability, determined whether projects, negotiations, and milestones succeeded or fell apart.

As a litigator, I saw how fear of confrontation, often dressed up as professionalism, turned minor disagreements into full-blown legal disputes. I watched leaders avoid honest conversations in the name of diplomacy, only to escalate tensions that could have been resolved with five minutes of clarity.

I saw how vague language, excessive delegation, or passive-aggressive silence eroded trust until relationships were irreparable. In mediation rooms, ego disguised as authority shut down collaboration. People were more invested in being right than in getting issues resolved.

In construction law, the pressure only intensified. I saw brilliant professionals buckle under the weight of unclear direction, unresolved tension, and unspoken expectations. I saw skilled and intelligent leadership teams' fracture because of unhelpful behaviours left unchecked. I saw the sigh that silenced a voice, the comment that killed creativity, and the intention that never matched its impact.

These weren't bad leaders. They were just overwhelmed – unaware of how their behaviour, especially under stress, was shaping culture, performance, and trust long before outcomes showed up on paper.

Then, I saw something else. I saw the opposite.

I saw leaders who stayed calm in the storm not because they had all the answers but because they had presence. They listened before reacting, asked thoughtful questions, and didn't dominate to be trusted; their steadiness earned them respect.

These were the ones who brought clarity to chaos, who created safety in tension, and who inspired through consistency. That became my benchmark.

In time, I became that leader. The trusted advisor, the steady voice, the one others turned to when things felt like they might fall apart. My progress didn't come from just reading books or climbing a ladder. It came from doing the work, first on myself, then with others.

This is how the Shiftcode Model was born: a behavioural framework forged in real conflict, real collapse, and the real courage it takes to lead differently. Since that moment, my mission has been clear: to decode the behaviours that drive trust, collaboration, engagement, and inspiration and expose the ones that quietly destroy them.

Not with judgement but with clarity and compassion.

Across industries, hierarchies, and in cultural contexts, the patterns are the same: brilliant, smart, capable leaders fail because of their blind spots, the unexamined behaviours they've normalised, the habits they were never taught to question, and the micro-moments in their leadership that shape how others feel about the work, the culture, and themselves.

This book is about those blind spots. It's about the moments behind the scenes, the behaviours that shape your team, culture, and legacy every day.

The Shiftcode Model is my answer to that challenge. It is a behavioural navigation system combining two practical frameworks: the Shiftcode Quadrants and the Shiftcode Compass. Together, they give you a mirror, a map, and a method.

Tired of performative development? Done the courses, tried the models, and still feel like something is missing? Sense your team is capable of more, but something invisible keeps getting in the way?

If that's you, this is the reset you need – a call to lead from presence, build trust before strategy, and shift culture through behaviour. In these pages, you'll find stories, practices, and frameworks to support you on your journey, and, above all, you'll find yourself.

You don't need a bigger title, a new job, or even to fix anyone else. You just need to shift your behaviour consistently, consciously, and courageously.

This is a leadership practice, and your shift starts now.

Introduction

Who is a leader? What makes a great one? Leadership has never been about the title on your door or how many people report to you. It's not about being the loudest in the room or the smartest in the meeting. It's about how you show up, especially when no one's watching. Strong leadership is reflected in your presence, your posture, and the small, consistent behaviours that shape the experiences of those around you. Every day, whether you're aware of it or not, you are setting the tone. That's leadership. Yes, it counts, even when things are rocky.

Many people in leadership roles have been told that knowledge and experience are the ultimate keys to success – but knowing isn't leading. You can have an MBA, two decades of experience, and a bulletproof strategy and still leave a trail of disengaged teams, confused communication, and missed opportunities, because leadership is about how you show up.

The possibility gap

If you've ever sat in a room and thought, *With all this talent, why aren't we getting better results?* or walked away from a meeting sensing something important was left unsaid, you've felt it: the discomfort of knowing your team is capable of more but not quite achieving it. That space between potential and performance is what I call the possibility gap. It's rarely caused by incompetence or lack of drive; it's almost always rooted in invisible misalignments, unclear expectations, and unconscious behavioural habits.

This isn't just a theoretical problem. According to Gallup, only 21% of employees felt truly engaged at work in 2024 (Cox, 2025). That might seem like a small dip from previous years, but in real-world terms, it cost the global economy over US$438 billion in lost productivity. That's a lot. No data set, report, or quarterly review can fix what behaviour breaks.

One of the reasons this gap continues to exist is because traditional leadership development simply hasn't kept up with new trends. Most leadership programmes are still designed around outdated assumptions and are focused on competencies, personality types, or abstract theories that never translate into positive daily behaviours. You go to a training, take notes, and feel energised, and two weeks later, nothing has changed. Why is this so?

Work is changing fast. Teams are more distributed, roles are more fluid, and expectations are higher than ever. The old top-down, command-and-control model? It doesn't inspire anyone anymore. People follow leaders who show up with clarity and consistency. Leaders who don't just manage outcomes but model the behaviours that drive them.

In 2014, when Satya Nadella took over as CEO of Microsoft, the company was stuck. Innovation had slowed, the culture had grown rigid, and silos dominated (Nadella, 2017). Internally, employees described the environment as hyper-competitive and guarded, with teams operating more like rivals than collaborators. Nadella didn't walk into the company with a sweeping strategy deck or a promise to revolutionise products. His first shift was behavioural. He began by listening, observing, asking questions, and, perhaps most importantly, being empathetic.

Nadella modelled a completely different kind of leadership. He wasn't the loudest voice in the room and didn't lead with control. He led with care. Slowly, the ripple effects began. Teams stopped competing and started collaborating. Innovation returned, and revenue soared. The shift wasn't in the company's software; it was in its behaviour. With Nadella's leadership style, Microsoft became more human.

Stories like this remind us that leadership is about presence, posture, and the thousand micro-moments that shape how others feel in your orbit. That's the kind of leadership this book invites you into.

Real leadership isn't shaped in conference rooms or by watching slide decks; it's forged in real-time moments. The ones where you pause before reacting. Where you give feedback that invites growth instead of shame. Where you make space for clarity when confusion creeps in.

When leaders don't take the time to reflect on how they're showing up, patterns repeat themselves. Teams check out, the high performers burn out, good ideas stay bottled up, and trust quietly erodes. You know the scariest part? Most leaders never realise that they've become the common denominator.

I've seen it happen time and time again. Leaders across construction, finance, education, tech – you name it. Smart and capable people stuck in unconscious habits that pull their teams further away from possibility.

A new model for positive change

I've been there too. Earlier in my career, I was a construction lawyer. I thrived in fast-paced environments, prided myself on getting things done, and could power through almost anything. I could lead tough negotiations, draft perfect contracts, and successfully manage complex deals. What I didn't see, however, or should I say, what I wasn't trained to see, was how fear and perfectionism shaped the way I showed up. I didn't understand how often I led from pressure instead of purpose. How I buried my discomfort instead of addressing it. How those patterns, invisible as they seemed, had clear consequences for the people around me.

I had a turning point, and no, it didn't come from getting a promotion or taking a course. It came from burnout, from getting honest feedback I didn't want to hear, and from seeing the gap between the leader I thought I was and the one I actually was. That gap didn't close overnight. It took curiosity, courage, and a complete shift in how I thought about behaviour. That's when the Shiftcode Model was born. I created it to help myself (initially) and other leaders navigate their turning points and lead with more awareness and purpose.

Today, as a certified emotional intelligence facilitator and mindfulness practitioner, I support leaders across industries in developing the power skills that create hard results. Empathy, presence, self-regulation, and active listening are essential skills in a world where change is constant and connection matters more than ever.

The world needs a new kind of leadership. We're living in a time of increasing complexity, rapid transformation, and unprecedented pressure. The old models of top-down control and charisma-driven leadership no longer work. People are no longer inspired by titles but by trust. They don't want perfection – they want presence. They don't want to be managed – they want to be led.

The Shiftcode Model meets this moment. It's a practical and behaviour-first guide that helps leaders shift in real time. At its core, the Shiftcode Model is a behaviour-based leadership model designed to close the gap between potential and performance. It offers two simple, powerful frameworks. The first is the Shiftcode Quadrants, which is your diagnostic lens for understanding your default leadership state.

The second is the Shiftcode Compass. This is a behavioural GPS that orients your daily actions around four essential codes. These four internal codes form the foundation of leadership excellence. As well as helping you reflect, they help you shift.

How this book will help

When leaders begin to shift, even in small ways, everything changes. I've trained burned-out leaders to rediscover energy, and I've helped mid-level managers transform their teams by simply learning how to listen differently. One small shift, like speaking expectations aloud instead of assuming them, can create space for innovation, ownership, and alignment to grow. These shifts are simple, but they are far from easy. That's why this book exists.

This isn't just another leadership book filled with nice quotes and forgettable tips. This is a practical guide, a call to action for leaders who want to show up differently and create teams that excel. Through reading this book, you'll identify habits that have been holding you back from becoming an excellent leader. You'll move through patterns like assumption, avoidance, and inconsistency and replace them with awareness, accountability, and intentionality.

Leadership today demands courage. The courage to lead yourself first, to see what you don't want to see, and to shift your behaviour so others have permission to do the same. Here, you'll learn all that it takes to lead in today's world.

This book is for anyone who's ever felt the tension between the leader they are and the leader they aspire to be. Whether you're a seasoned executive craving deeper impact, a new manager finding your footing, or an emerging leader ready to grow, you'll find guidance here. It's also for those who understand that leadership is defined not by a title, but by presence, behaviour, and intention.

If you've ever delivered results but felt disconnected from your team, questioned your ability to inspire despite external praise, or struggled to consistently embody the leader you want to be, this book is for you.

More than a framework, leadership excellence is a mirror to see yourself clearly, a map to guide your growth, and a call to practise leadership in a way that feels real and impactful. Whether you're leading a team, influencing an organisation, or navigating personal change, this book will help you lead with greater awareness, authenticity, and purpose.

When you shift, the ripple effect is extraordinary. Culture changes, teams thrive, and you begin leading from the place where your influence is most powerful, which is your behaviour.

Let's get into it by decoding the behaviours that are holding you back and unlocking the ones that will move you and your team forward.

PART ONE
THE STRUGGLES FOR LEADERSHIP EXCELLENCE

What if the real challenge in leadership is more than capability? What if what we really need is clarity?

Leadership isn't failing because of a lack of tools, titles, or training. It's failing because of invisible gaps, which are subtle disconnects between what leaders intend and how their teams experience them. These gaps don't appear overnight; they are shaped by the changing workplace ecosystems, where hybrid models blur boundaries, generational differences fuel miscommunication, and burnout, blame, and disconnection quietly spread like smoke through the culture.

Part One of this book discusses those hidden spaces where leadership excellence breaks down – the possibility gaps. They are the missed opportunities where trust could have been built but wasn't. Where collaboration could have thrived but collapsed. Where inspiration could have flowed, but instead, disengagement took its place.

Before you can shift how you lead, you need to first understand where you truly stand.

ONE

You Think You're Leading, But Are You?

A leader walks into a room, armed with clarity, confidence, and conviction. They believe they're modelling integrity, building trust, inspiring excellence, and steering their team towards collective success. Their calendar is full, their meetings are productive, and their intentions are clear.

After they leave, however, the silence in the room says everything. Attention drifts, engagement dips, conversations become guarded, and innovation stalls. Beneath the surface, something important is happening. While their leadership is being felt, it's not in the way they intended. They thought they were leading but they were only managing perceptions.

Modern leadership has evolved. It's no longer about how polished your strategy is, how many metrics you've mastered, or how impressive your track record looks on paper. Leadership today lives in the emotional spaces between people, including how safe they feel, how seen they are, and how inspired they become through your presence.

It's the difference between *doing* leadership and *being* a leader. An uncomfortable truth is that we can't see ourselves leading. We can only see our effort, our intent, our logic, and our justifications. Others experience something different: our tone, our timing, our tension, and our blind spots. Where we believe we are empowering, they may feel overpowered. Where we think we are clear, they may feel confused. Where we feel composed, they may sense distance.

Your team doesn't work with your intentions. It works with your impact, because real leadership begins with self-awareness, with having the courage to explore the gap between how you think you lead and how you are experienced. That gap is where culture is built, trust is either nurtured or eroded, and leadership either transforms or falls short.

Research shows that self-awareness is a critical component of effective leadership. A study by Korn Ferry found that self-awareness was the strongest predictor of overall leadership success (2013). Yet, according to Dr Tasha Eurich, an organisational psychologist and author of *Insight*, while 95% of people think they're self-aware, only 10% to 15% actually are (2017). That gap between perception and reality is where leadership often falls apart. Leaders who understand their strengths, weaknesses, and the impact of their behaviour on others are more successful in their roles.

Bill George, former Medtronic CEO and author of *True North*, emphasises that authentic leadership begins with being self-aware (2007). He argues that leaders who are grounded in their values and are aware of their triggers and tendencies build more genuine relationships. It's no coincidence that some of the world's most respected leaders, like Jacinda Ardern, Satya Nadella, and Barack Obama, are known not just for what they do, but for how people feel in their presence. Their leadership lives in the emotional residue they leave behind.

Before we talk about KPIs, scalable transformation, or strategic frameworks, we need to confront the deeper and often avoided question: are you really leading or just managing intentions? If you're willing to honestly sit with this question, then everything else becomes possible.

In this opening chapter, we will look into the critical distinction between leadership intentions and actual impact. We'll discuss why, although many leaders believe they're effectively guiding their teams, their actions may not resonate as intended. By the end of this chapter, you'll understand the importance of aligning your leadership approach with the experiences of your team.

The hidden gap between intent and impact

Most leaders set out to make a difference, to lead with purpose and to drive results and bring out the best in others. Somewhere along the way, however, something gets lost.

You give what you think is a motivating message, but your team hears pressure. You believe you're empowering people, but they feel abandoned. You think you're calm under pressure, but others see you as cold or unapproachable.

This is the silent and often dangerous gap between intent and impact. It's the space where even well-meaning leadership efforts go off course. It's about the mismatch between how we see ourselves and how others experience us. In leadership, that mismatch carries weight because it's not your intentions that shape team culture; it's your behaviour.

This is what Harvard Business School professor Dr Amy Edmondson calls the 'shadow side' of leadership: the unintended consequences of our leadership actions (2018). Edmondson, best known for her work on psychological safety, highlights how even the most experienced leaders can undermine their teams when they're not mindful of how their behaviour lands. Her research shows that psychological safety, which is how safe people feel to speak up, admit mistakes, or offer dissenting opinions, is a stronger predictor of high-performing teams than talent or tenure.

The modern workplace is full of leaders who are exhausted, well-intentioned, and confused as to why things still feel like they're falling apart – such as why morale is low, collaboration is stalling, and trust is slipping through their fingers. The truth is that many are caught in this invisible gap, basing their leadership on internal clarity but not on external resonance.

Leadership without self-awareness is a risk

Leadership is defined not by what you intend to do but by what others experience as a result of your presence and decisions. You may intend to give constructive feedback, but if your tone is defensive, your team member will walk away discouraged. You may intend to model resilience, but if you never show vulnerability, your team will interpret it as emotional distance. You may intend to foster collaboration, but if you dominate meetings, you will unintentionally silence contributions.

Your intent lives in your mind, and your impact lives in your team's experience. When those two don't align, confusion and disconnection take root.

According to Dr Brené Brown, renowned researcher and author of *Dare to Lead*, clarity is kindness (2018). When leaders communicate with ambiguity, even if well-intentioned, they create space for assumptions, fear, and disengagement. Her research on vulnerability and leadership shows that we connect with others not through perfection, but through presence.

Why does the gap exist?

The gap between intent and impact runs deeper than just a communication problem. It is often fuelled by:

- Unconscious habits – patterns developed over time that operate on autopilot. For example, a leader who interrupts team members mid-sentence because they're eager to add value, not realising they're actually silencing voices and creating a culture where people stop contributing ideas.

- Unspoken assumptions – beliefs about what good leadership should look like. For instance, assuming that being decisive means making quick decisions without input, when your team actually interprets this as being dismissive of their expertise and excluding them from important choices.

- Emotional residue – feelings and thoughts from past experiences, including stress, wounds, or self-doubt – that distort your behaviour in high-stakes moments.

- Cultural wiring – experiences and activities, such as childhood lessons, societal norms, or professional conditioning – that shape your instincts. For instance, if you were raised in a culture that values hierarchy and deference to authority, you might struggle to create psychological safety where team members feel comfortable challenging your ideas or admitting mistakes.

For example, if you were taught that showing emotion is a weakness, you may lead with excessive control. If your early career rewarded performance over presence, you may neglect team dynamics in pursuit of outcomes. If you grew up navigating conflict with silence, you may now avoid difficult conversations entirely.

These internalised behaviours don't make you a bad leader – that's just you being human – but when left unchecked, they become costly.

When intent isn't enough

A senior executive once said during a mentoring session, 'I don't get it; I tell them I care. I give them freedom. But they say I'm hard to approach and I don't listen.'

He wasn't lying. He truly believed he was being supportive, but his impact told another story. His team saw someone who checked in only when problems arose, who rushed conversations, and who praised results but ignored effort. To them, it felt like distance, disinterest, and even dismissal.

That's the thing about leadership. Your good intentions don't protect you from unintended harm. When people experience misalignment between what you say and how they feel around you, they begin to doubt your authenticity. Over time, trust erodes, engagement slips, and communication shuts down. Not because you didn't care, but because you didn't see the gap.

In boating terms, your 'wake' is the trail you leave behind. Leadership is no different. Every interaction leaves a trail of energy, emotion, and memory. You may move on from a team meeting, but your team carries the feeling you left behind. You may forget a passing comment, but someone else replays it for weeks. You may think silence is safe, but others interpret it as neglect.

Leadership expert Marshall Goldsmith puts it plainly in his book *What Got You Here Won't Get You There*: the habits and behaviours that made you successful in one context can become blind spots in another (2007). Without feedback, reflection, and a willingness to change, you risk leading in a vacuum.

The first shift in leadership excellence is to start measuring your impact as well as your intent, because a leadership role is made up of a series of ripples.

The real cost of behavioural blind spots

Imagine trying to steer a ship while looking through a fogged window. You see fragments, distorted shapes, and a vague outline of the direction you're going in, but you miss the full picture. That's what it's like to lead with behavioural blind spots.

Of course, you're navigating, showing up, and making decisions, but without clear visibility, you're relying on instinct instead of awareness. Often, you don't realise the damage you're causing until something crashes.

We all have blind spots. If you're thinking, *Well, not me*, that's probably your first one. Blind spots are the unconscious behaviours, habits, and emotional reactions that you don't notice but that others experience daily. They're shaped by your upbringing, culture, personality, past experiences, and even trauma. They're the default scripts running in the background while you're focused on trying to be a good leader.

Make no mistake. These unseen behaviours shape how you lead, how you're perceived, and how people feel around you.

Behavioural blind spots are patterns you're usually unaware of, but that influence every corner of your leadership. They affect how you:

- Make decisions under pressure

- Respond to conflict or criticism

- Communicate with direct reports

- Interpret team dynamics

- Create or destroy psychological safety

They're sneaky and can masquerade as strengths or good intentions. For example:

- You interrupt team members and tell yourself it's just 'passion'.

- You avoid giving hard feedback and call it 'protecting morale'.

- You micromanage and label it 'being thorough'.

- You emotionally detach and call it 'professionalism'.

Do any of these sound familiar? If not in yourself, then probably in someone you've worked with. They aren't always conscious choices. They're usually inherited behaviours – protective, habitual, and deeply rooted responses you've learned over time – and they've helped you survive in tough environments. Leadership isn't about surviving, though. It's about seeing clearly and choosing consciously.

Why we all have them

Blind spots aren't flaws. They're functions of human adaptation. From a young age, we learn to behave in ways that help us stay safe, accepted, and successful in the environments we're in. These coping mechanisms get internalised, and by the time we're leading others, they've become part of how we operate.

Think about it. Were you raised to be polite and honest? Then you might avoid confrontation and think you're being respectful due to cultural conditioning. Did your first boss reward overwork and discourage emotion? You might now lead with task urgency but overlook your team's emotional signals due to early work experiences. Have you been burned by feedback before? You might unconsciously shut down when someone pushes back, due to personal wounds.

While this doesn't mean you're unfit to lead, you still need to examine your blind spots, as they're the ones driving your leadership. They come with a cost.

Let's leave theory for a bit and focus on practice. The following three examples illustrate workplace moments – drawn from experiences and stories shared in coaching sessions, exit interviews, and leadership reflections – and have been anonymised to highlight the patterns, not the people.

1. Project derailment due to reactive leadership

Raj was known as a rockstar project manager. He was smart, fast, and reliable. When his team's product launch hit a snag, Raj rolled up his sleeves, stayed late, jumped into Slack channels, and rewrote timelines, all in the name of helping.

Behind the scenes, however, his team felt differently. They felt smothered and micromanaged. One person said, 'It's like he stopped trusting us.' Another started holding back ideas, afraid of being overruled.

The product launched late, not because they weren't capable, but because collaboration had collapsed under the weight of Raj's reactivity. His blind spot is urgency. As a child, Raj learned that showing up fast meant you cared, but in the workplace context, it translated as anxiety, not support. The cost of Raj's blind spot was that it eroded trust, stifled collaboration, and caused emotional burnout in a high-performing team.

2. Toxic team culture from a well-intentioned but unaware leader

Emily was warm, friendly, and new to leadership. She genuinely wanted everyone to feel good at work, so when two team members started butting heads over shared responsibilities, Emily did nothing. She smiled, changed the subject, and hoped it would pass. Well, it didn't.

Tension turned into gossip, and resentment built. One of the team members quit, citing 'a hostile work environment'. Emily was shocked. She'd never yelled, she celebrated birthdays, and she always said thank you.

Emily's blind spot is conflict avoidance dressed as kindness. Her refusal to engage was interpreted as indifference. Her niceness gave dysfunction a green light. The cost was a loss of a valuable team member, a loss of team trust, and a silent endorsement of toxicity.

3. Silence in conflict

Daniel was admired as an emotionally intelligent leader – he read Dr Brené Brown and encouraged open dialogue – but when a cross-functional conflict erupted between two departments, Daniel froze. He told himself, 'They're adults. They'll figure it out.' Without his leadership, the conflict increased. Emails became passive-aggressive, collaboration vanished, and productivity plummeted.

Daniel's blind spot is avoiding discomfort under the guise of maturity. In his family, conflict meant disconnection, so he stayed neutral, and in doing so, he vanished when it mattered most. The cost was team fragmentation, missed opportunities for resolution, and erosion of confidence in leadership.

Let's be real. These stories reflect patterns we've all seen in organisations: the leader who *preaches openness* yet shuts down opposing views, the manager who *demands results* but overlooks effort, glossing over disagreements in the mistaken belief that harmony comes from avoidance, and the executive who claims to put *people first* but avoids eye contact and retreats from conflict rather than stepping into it.

These aren't bad people. They're well-intentioned leaders with blind spots. Over time, these blind spots create leadership disconnects like trust breaking down, engagement withering, innovation disappearing, and culture curdling.

The worst part is that most leaders never see it happening. People rarely challenge a leader's blind spot. They disengage quietly, comply without care, and leave without explanation.

A 2021 study by MIT Sloan found that toxic work culture, not pay, is the strongest predictor of attrition (Sull, 2022). Toxicity is often the by-product of unexamined leadership behaviours.

The real cost of blind spots is the distance between your good intentions and your team's lived reality. It's the gap where trust leaks, performance dips, and connection fades. Unless you're brave enough to look in the fogged-up mirror, you'll never close that gap.

Common leadership disconnects

Blind spots rarely crash through the front door. They slip in through the side, unnoticed, quiet, and almost polite. They don't make a scene or demand attention. Instead, they show up in the margins of meetings, in the silence after feedback, and in the slight hesitation before someone speaks up.

When left unchecked, blind spots widen. What begins as a small disconnect grows into a chasm between what a leader intends and how they are experienced, between the values on the wall and the behaviours in the room, and between potential and reality.

This is where good intentions quietly show up. It's not usually one big moment that breaks leadership credibility. It's a series of small moments where alignment was lost, and no one noticed until something gave way.

Let's discuss the three most common and costly leadership disconnects that we see playing out again and again, with illustrative examples. Not because leaders don't care, but because leadership, at its core, is relational and not rational.

Trust erosion: Missed collaboration opportunities

Trust is the operating system within a team. When trust is high, things flow. People share openly, challenge respectfully, support willingly, and innovate freely. When it begins to erode even subtly, everything costs more: time, effort, clarity, and morale.

Nina, a senior director at a rapidly scaling fintech startup, was admired for her calm demeanour and belief in hiring top-tier talent. She prided herself on being hands-off. She trusted her team, and in her mind, that trust meant giving them space, so she rarely checked in unless there was a problem.

At first, her team appreciated the autonomy, but over time, something changed. Without Nina's visible support, cross-functional projects lost momentum. When challenges emerged, team members hesitated to ask for help, unsure if Nina was truly available. A few interpreted her distance as disinterest. Others felt like they were working in a vacuum.

What Nina thought was empowering felt, to her team, like abandonment. This resulted in collaboration stalling, silos forming, and innovation becoming territorial. The autonomy that was meant to foster excellence had quietly brought isolation.

Nina's blind spot is equating distance with empowerment. The cost of her blind spot was a breakdown in cross-team trust, missed opportunities for synergy, and an innovation culture that plateaued.

According to Google's Project Aristotle, psychological safety, the shared belief that a team is safe for interpersonal risk-taking, emerged as the single most important predictor of team success (Duhigg, 2016). That safety is built, in part, through the visible presence of leadership.

Nina didn't intend to be absent – she thought she was being respectful – but the lack of connection sent a louder message than she realised.

Disengagement: Productivity loss

Disengagement doesn't always look like defiance. It often wears a mask of politeness, routine, and compliance.

Kevin was a performance-driven team leader in a corporate sales division. His meetings were efficient, his dashboards immaculate, and his standards high. He made it clear that results mattered; KPIs were his language. Over time, team participation dwindled, idea-sharing dried up, and people started doing only what was required, no more, no less. Absenteeism rose, and the energy in the room became stale.

Kevin couldn't understand it. The numbers were being met (although barely), but the momentum was gone. He was doing everything he'd been taught: set clear goals, track metrics, and push for performance.

What he missed was that his team didn't feel seen as people. There were no check-ins that asked 'How are you really?' There was no curiosity about their motivations, their blocks, their aspirations. It was all output and no connection.

Kevin's blind spot is valuing performance over people. The cost was diminished engagement, a compliance culture over a commitment culture, and gradual erosion of creative thinking and initiative.

According to Gallup's 2020 research, business units with high employee engagement tend to be about 21% more profitable than less engaged ones. When your people feel seen, supported, and cared for, that commitment translates into better performance and a customer experience that truly reflects your values.

Lack of inspiration: Innovation stifled

Inspiration isn't just the stuff of TED Talks and annual off-sites. It's the heartbeat of motivation, especially in seasons of change, pressure, and ambiguity.

Tariq was a senior executive at a global consulting firm. He was a brilliant strategist and a razor-sharp thinker, and had a reputation for turning around underperforming departments. He also believed in letting data do the talking. To Tariq, inspiration was fluff. People should be self-motivated because they have jobs to do.

After a year filled with restructures, budget cuts, and long hours, however, his team were depleted. They weren't just tired; they were disillusioned. They weren't looking for fireworks or lofty speeches; they were looking for meaning, for context, and for a reason to care.

Tariq's updates were always practical, to the point, and impersonal. No stories or vision. Just targets and timelines. Eventually, his team stopped contributing beyond the basics. Innovation dropped, and no one wanted to speak up or stretch themselves.

Tariq's blind spot is believing that strategy is enough. The cost was emotional disconnect from vision, low morale in the face of change, and a culture of passivity instead of proactive leadership.

A report by McKinsey & Company found that leaders who balance competence with compassion, strategy with inspiration, foster higher levels of loyalty and performance (D'Auria, 2020). In tough times, inspiration is the fuel that keeps the fire alive.

What do Nina, Kevin, and Tariq have in common?

They weren't careless or malicious – they were good leaders with good intentions – but each missed the disconnect between their intent and their impact. They paid for it in trust, performance, and culture.

That's the scary thing about leadership disconnects: they don't scream but whisper. As a result, the boldest team member starts holding back, the most creative voice becomes silent, and the high performer begins looking elsewhere.

The leader, caught up in strategy or structure or survival, doesn't see it happening, because blind spots usually show up in a team's energy. If something feels off but you can't quite name it, don't ignore that instinct. That's often the signal that a disconnect is already at work.

CASE STUDY: The project collapse

Let's zoom in on what blind spots look like in action, and what they can truly cost when left unchecked.

Background

A mid-sized consultancy firm landed a major contract: a AU$4.2 million client implementation with a high-stakes three-month deadline. With full C-suite visibility and reputation on the line, this was a make-or-break opportunity.

Leading the project was Alex, a senior manager with a stellar record. Technically sharp, intensely driven, and laser-focused on delivery, Alex seemed like the ideal candidate. Underneath the accolades and experience, however, he carried unexamined behavioural patterns: blind spots that would quietly unravel the project.

Week 1: The invisible start line

Alex launched straight into execution. No kick-off meeting, no shared vision, and no team huddle. He believed the documentation was self-explanatory and expected everyone to get on with it, but clarity on paper doesn't guarantee shared understanding. Within days, deliverables overlapped, responsibilities blurred, and assumptions clashed.

Alex's blind spot here was assuming clarity instead of creating it. The result was misaligned priorities, duplicated work, and mounting tension from day one.

Week 3: Control versus Collaboration

As problems surfaced, Alex did what he thought any responsible leader would do, which was to tighten the reins. He started micromanaging tasks, scrutinising every detail, and firing off late-night emails. Some team members were dropped from key meetings. Others stopped contributing, retreating emotionally while still showing up physically.

His blind spot was mistaking urgency and control for leadership. He believed speed was the solution, unaware that it was reinforcing the dysfunction. The result was diminished ownership, disengaged talent, and a culture of quiet resentment.

Week 6: Conflict avoidance

When a conflict erupted between two leads, one from operations, the other from development, it was a chance to reset and realign. Alex avoided it. He told himself, 'They're smart people, they'll find a way to work it out.' He stayed silent, hoping it would blow over. Well, it didn't.

Instead, resentment festered. The tension spread across sub-teams, infecting collaboration and creating a culture of avoidance.

Alex's blind spot in this context was avoiding emotional discomfort. Conflict felt threatening, so he bypassed it, allowing disconnection to grow unchecked. The result was broken communication, eroded trust, and irreversible fractures in team dynamics.

Week 10: The fallout

The client had seen enough. Mixed messages, repeated delays, and low visibility prompted an escalation to the C-suite. One week later, the contract was cancelled. What was meant to be the firm's flagship success turned into an internal case study in what not to do.

Three team members resigned, others quietly updated their résumés, and the reputational hit lingered far beyond the project's timeline.

In exit interviews, the same feedback echoed: 'We didn't feel heard', 'There was no real leadership', 'It was chaos'.

Alex wanted to succeed. He was invested, competent, and committed, but his unchecked blind spots created a leadership vacuum. Your success as a leader is ultimately defined by what your team experiences.

Post-mortem: The hidden cost of blind spots

The table below reveals how blind spots translate into specific leadership behaviours, and their cascading effects on team performance. Each blind spot follows a predictable pattern: unconscious behaviour leads to leadership action, which creates unintended consequences.

Behavioural Blind Spot	Leadership Action	Unfavourable Outcome
Assumed clarity	Skipped team alignment	Disengagement, reduced ownership
Reactive control	Micromanagement	Confusion, misaligned tasks
Conflict avoidance	Silence during tensions	Breakdown of team trust and collaboration
Overconfidence in expertise	Dismissed team feedback	Resistance to course-correct, project loss

The true cost

Alex's blind spots led to:

- Financial loss of AU$4.2 million
- Team turnover leading to three resignations and multiple disengaged contributors

The cultural impact

The impact of Alex's blind spots was trust erosion, lowered morale, and a dented internal brand.

It wasn't one action that led to the collapse. It was a pattern, a series of small but significant misalignments between intent and impact, stacked over time.

EXERCISE: Five powerful questions to uncover your leadership possibility gaps

Before we move forward, let's pause and make space for self-inquiry – the kind that illuminates blind spots before they show up in costly ways.

The following questions are meant to stir something on a deep level. You might want to journal your thoughts or discuss them with a coach or trusted peer. Come back to them often. Your answers will evolve with your leadership.

1. Where do your good intentions create unintended outcomes? (Think about a moment when you felt misunderstood, or when things didn't land as expected.)

2. What behaviours have you normalised that might be undermining trust or engagement? (Consider patterns you notice when you're under pressure. Do you withdraw? Do you control? Do you avoid?)

3. Whose voices do you listen to most, and who might you unintentionally silence or overlook? (Reflect on inclusion, influence, and your internal circle.)

4. When was the last time you asked for feedback on your leadership and truly listened without defending yourself? (Receiving feedback well is a leadership skill in itself.)

5. If your team described your leadership behind closed doors, what might they say, and what do you hope they would say? (Be honest when answering this. This gap is your work.)

Self-awareness is the foundation for behavioural intelligence, the ability to align your inner world with your outer impact. When your behaviours align with your values, you build trust. When trust is present, performance follows.

That's the heart of the Shiftcode Model. It isn't a quick-fix model, but a personal leadership GPS you follow when you're willing to course-correct.

The gap between intention and impact is where most leadership struggles begin and where transformation is most possible. When we overlook our behavioural blind spots, we risk eroding the trust and connection we're trying to build; when we start paying attention, even small shifts can unlock extraordinary results.

Leadership excellence begins with self-awareness, but it doesn't end there. In the next chapter, we'll discuss why behaviour, not just knowledge or intention, is the true driver of results. You'll see how your day-to-day habits either build or break the outcomes you're working so hard to achieve.

Stay with me.

TWO
Behaviours Drive Results

W alk into any organisation during performance-review season, and you'll likely hear the same tired refrains echoing through the halls: 'We need to hit our targets', 'Let's adjust the strategy', 'We should run another training session'.

Sound familiar?

In the corporate world, we're conditioned to chase results by tweaking plans, upgrading tools, or adding more knowledge. We equate high performance with intelligence, process, and expertise. While those things matter, they're not what drives transformation – because if knowledge alone were the answer, organisations filled with brilliant minds wouldn't be struggling, leaders wouldn't feel stuck, teams wouldn't stall, and cultures wouldn't collapse under pressure.

Shockingly, they do. All the time. Because the true engine behind sustainable results isn't found in strategy decks or skills matrices. It's found in people's daily behaviours: how they show up in tough conversations, how they respond to failure, how they collaborate under pressure, and how they treat one another when no one's watching. That's the missing link: the behavioural gap.

It's not the big leadership moments that make or break performance; it's the small, repeated ones. The micro-behaviours that either build trust or chip away at it. The subtle cues that make a space psychologically safe or stifling.

In this chapter, we're shifting the spotlight away from knowledge gaps and personality traits. We're moving on to what really drives results: behaviour. This is the way people act, interact, and react in real time.

Why knowing isn't leading

One of the most persistent myths in leadership is the belief that knowledge automatically translates into behaviour. That if someone understands what good leadership looks like, has read the books, attended the training programmes and the workshops, and absorbed the frameworks, they will naturally lead well. Time and time again, we see this isn't true.

Think about it. How many leaders do you know who can quote Simon Sinek on purpose, Dr Brené Brown on vulnerability, or Dr Daniel Goleman on emotional intelligence, but nevertheless lead with impatience, distance, or control when under pressure? They've got the language, they've got the learning, but when it really matters, their actions don't align. Why? Because knowing something and living it are two different things.

Leadership is a practice. It's not what you say or believe that shapes how your team experiences you; it's how you behave when the stakes are high, the pressure is on, and the spotlight isn't there. That's the moment when real leadership shows up or doesn't.

We've seen it happen in organisations of all sizes. A senior manager completes an expensive leadership programme. They're enthusiastic, articulate, and intellectually engaged with everything they've learned. They know how to talk about psychological safety and inclusive leadership. Back at work, though, when a junior team member raises a dissenting opinion, they shut it down with a curt 'Let's not go down that rabbit hole.' No discussion and no curiosity. Just business as usual.

It's not that they didn't *know* better. It's that they didn't *do* better. That gap, which is the space between intellectual understanding and behavioural consistency, is where so many leaders struggle. Often, they don't even realise it's happening, because in their mind, the intent is there. The knowledge is there. What's missing? What's missing is integration.

Awareness isn't transformation

This is what I usually refer to as the knowing-doing disconnect. This is a common leadership pitfall where individuals mistake awareness for transformation. They assume that because they understand a concept, it must show up in their actions. As we have seen, leadership impact isn't measured by what you know, however. It's measured by how your team experiences you.

In psychology, it is called the intention-behaviour gap: a well-documented phenomenon that shows how even when people intend to act differently, their behaviours often remain unchanged. It's not because they're lying or lazy. It's because behavioural patterns are sticky. They're shaped by years of reinforcement and emotional conditioning.

Here's a relatable example.

During a coaching engagement, a client, let's call her Laila, shared that she'd just completed a six-month leadership accelerator. She felt more confident, informed, and 'ready to lead differently'. When her team completed a feedback survey shortly after, however, the results were disappointing. Many said they still felt hesitant to speak up. Several described her as intense or hard to read. One person noted that although she talked more about inclusion, the meetings still felt dominated by her voice.

Laila was shocked. 'But I've been trying so hard,' she said. 'I've changed the way I lead.'

When we dug further, it became clear: Laila had changed the way she talked about leadership, but she hadn't yet changed her micro-behaviours, which include the eye contact, the pauses, the tone, and the space she gave others to speak. Her good intentions and intellectual knowledge hadn't yet made the journey into her daily actions – and her team could feel it.

This isn't unusual. It's why knowledge, while essential, is never sufficient.

Think about the health world. Everyone knows that exercising regularly, drinking water, and sleeping well are good for the body, but how many people do these things consistently? It's not about information. It's about behaviour, and leadership is no different.

In a study published in the *Journal of Applied Psychology*, researchers found that leadership development programmes were far more effective when they included behavioural tracking and accountability mechanisms, not just content delivery (2017). In other words, the leaders who changed were the ones who focused on their habits, as well as their knowledge.

This aligns with Daniel Goleman's research on emotional intelligence in the workplace (1998). His studies reveal a critical gap: people can understand the principles of emotional intelligence yet still struggle to create trust or connection in real interactions. Why? Because it's not enough to know the qualities of emotional intelligence. You must practise them repeatedly, especially when it's hard.

The same applies to feedback. A leader may know that feedback should be timely, specific, and constructive. They may even coach others on how to do it. If, however, they still avoid uncomfortable conversations, sugarcoat messages to maintain harmony, and wait until review season to say what needed to be said months ago, then the knowledge hasn't become leadership. It's just theory. Knowing isn't leading. Showing up is.

The most powerful form of leadership is the kind that lives not just in your language, but also in your presence: in the way you listen, admit when you're wrong, and stay open when your ego wants to shut down. That's where leadership becomes real.

Ideas versus behaviour

It's worth noting that in many workplaces there's an unspoken hierarchy of value: ideas are celebrated more than behaviour. Articulating a vision gets more praise than embodying patience. Pitching a new initiative earns more visibility than consistently mentoring others. This creates a culture where knowledge is rewarded, but behavioural maturity is overlooked – but that's changing.

As organisations struggle with burnout, complexity, and generational shifts in values, they're realising that it's not just what leaders know that matters – it's what leaders model. Not what they say about culture, but what they do when it's tested. Not how much leadership theory they can quote, but how much emotional intelligence they can demonstrate under pressure.

The next time you find yourself saying, 'They should know better,' just pause. Maybe they do know better, but knowing is only half the story. Doing is the other half. It's the half that takes practice, reflection, and a willingness to get uncomfortable. Because leadership isn't built on information, it's built on integrity.

How patterns form and how to shift them

If you've ever found yourself repeating the same reaction, like snapping during stress, withdrawing when conflict arises, or over-explaining to prove your point, you're not alone. These aren't random occurrences, or bad habits and personality quirks. They're the result of behavioural patterns that have been formed, reinforced, and repeated over time.

At a glance, it might seem like our behaviour is the result of conscious choice, but most of what we do, especially in leadership, is shaped by forces beneath the surface. Behaviour is rarely about what we decide in the moment; it's more often about what we've practised, what we've adapted to, and what our brain has come to expect.

The science of behaviour

Neuroscience tells us that the brain is hardwired for efficiency. In other words, it doesn't want to work harder than it has to. It forms shortcuts, like habitual ways of thinking, feeling, and acting, that allow us to move through our day without analysing every choice. These shortcuts are useful when we're driving, brushing our teeth, or tying our shoes. They can become problematic, however, when they influence how we respond to feedback, handle emotional discomfort, or manage a high-stakes conversation with our team.

Think of your behaviour as being like a well-worn path in a forest. The more you walk that path, the clearer and more automatic it becomes. The more automatic it becomes, the less likely you are to question it. That's how behavioural patterns are formed – through repeated responses that become neurologically ingrained. These patterns are efficient, but they're not always effective.

Take, for example, a leader who grew up in a home where mistakes were met with criticism. Over time, they learn to associate failure with danger. Fast-forward twenty years: now they're in a senior leadership role, but that early emotional blueprint still exists in the background. Even without realising it, they might avoid admitting mistakes, lash out when something goes wrong, or demand perfection from their team. Unwittingly, the past becomes present through behaviour, because their behaviour follows a script written years ago.

This is where the concept of behavioural conditioning comes in. BF Skinner, one of the most influential behavioural psychologists of the twentieth century, explained that behaviours are shaped by their consequences. If a particular action is rewarded, whether with praise, safety, or relief, it becomes more likely to be repeated. If it's punished, through shame, rejection, or loss, it's likely to be suppressed.

In leadership, this plays out constantly. A manager who gets rewarded for 'always being right' might become addicted to control. A team member who once got burned for speaking up might learn to stay quiet, even when they know something's wrong. Behaviour becomes less about logic and more about safety.

What complicates things further is how behaviour becomes reinforced by both external rewards and internal sensations. Neuroscientist Dr Joe Dispenza talks about how repeated thoughts and emotions create a kind of biological memory. We literally become chemically addicted to our emotional states, whether that's anxiety, urgency, defensiveness, or even chaos. Even when a behaviour is unhelpful, therefore, it can still feel familiar. In the brain's operating system, familiar often equals safe.

This is why so many leaders find themselves stuck in cycles they don't fully understand. They know they don't want to micromanage. They know they should be more empathetic. They understand the value of listening. Their behaviour tells a different story, especially when stress is high and pressure is mounting. It's not because they lack willpower. It's because the default wiring kicks in before reflection can even begin.

The impact of stress

The link between stress and behaviour is particularly important. Under pressure, the brain shifts from its executive functions (logic, planning, and emotional regulation) to survival mode. The amygdala, which is the part of the brain responsible for fear responses, floods the system, narrowing our perspective. We see fewer options, interpret things more defensively, and revert to well-rehearsed coping mechanisms. In other words, the moments that demand our best leadership are the ones most likely to trigger our worst habits.

Let's consider this workplace pattern. In a company I observed, one of the most brilliant partners, let's call her Mira, had a habit of taking over team discussions when timelines got tight. To her, it felt like efficiency, but to her team, it felt like domination. She didn't intend to disempower people, but under pressure, her behavioural loop activated: take control, do it yourself, and move fast. It was an unconscious attempt to reduce risk.

When we zoom out, we can see what's happening clearly, but in the moment, we're not zoomed out. We're inside the pattern, reacting from muscle memory rather than from mindful choice.

There's also a cultural layer to all of this. Behavioural patterns are inherited and absorbed from the systems we grow up in. Family dynamics, school environments, religious teachings, and early professional mentors contribute to what we believe is normal, professional, or acceptable. For instance, if you grew up in a culture that discouraged emotional expression, you might now lead with distance and control, believing that it's what maturity looks like. If vulnerability was met with shame, you might avoid honest conversations, even when they're necessary.

Social learning theory, pioneered by psychologist Albert Bandura, reinforces this. As well as learning by doing, we learn by observing. The behaviours we see modelled in leadership shape what we come to internalise as effective, regardless of whether they're actually working.

This helps explain why even dysfunctional workplace cultures persist. If people get promoted by being aggressive, others learn to equate aggression with influence. If silence is rewarded more than candour, teams become risk-averse. If busyness is praised above balance, burnout becomes the norm. There is a pattern shaping culture.

How do we change?

While we'll discuss actionable tools and strategies in later chapters, it's important here to understand that change begins with awareness. The moment we recognise that what we've been calling our leadership style may actually be an inherited pattern, we begin to loosen its grip. Once that happens, new possibilities emerge.

Leaders who are willing to examine the origins of their behaviours, especially the ones they're most defensive about, start to access a different kind of influence – not one that's reactive or performative, but one that's grounded, responsive, and conscious.

Of course, none of this is fast. Behavioural patterns aren't broken just by reading a book or having a single a-ha moment. They're gradually unlearned through repeated choice, reflection, and practice. None of that is possible without first understanding the architecture of behaviour itself: how it forms, why it persists, and what makes it so resistant to change.

This is the invisible part of leadership that most performance reviews never touch. The subtle loops behind the scenes. The emotional history that shows up in our meetings. The well-meaning impulses that sabotage team cohesion. Until we understand this part, we'll keep over-relying on tactics and wondering why change doesn't stick, because strategy shifts nothing without behaviour, and behaviour doesn't shift without awareness.

That's why this work isn't just about being better. We need to recognise that the greatest leverage we have as leaders is in the small, repeated actions that reveal who we are, what we value, and what we've been rehearsing, often without knowing it.

The science is clear: what's been learned can be unlearned. First, it must be seen.

Behavioural intelligence drives results

If knowledge alone doesn't drive performance, and if unconscious patterns can quietly derail even the most well-meaning leaders, what creates sustained impact? The answer is behavioural intelligence. Not the kind of intelligence that shows up in degrees, certifications, or clever strategies, but the type that shows up in meetings, in conflict, and in feedback conversations. The kind that reveals itself in how a leader behaves when they're tired, triggered, or tested.

Behavioural intelligence is your moment-to-moment ability to recognise your default responses, regulate them, and choose behaviour that aligns with your intention, values, and the experience you want others to have. It's what turns insight into impact. It's what allows you to shift from reactivity to presence, and from presence to influence.

Behavioural intelligence is what gives leaders the ability to pause before reacting. To create space between stimulus and response. To observe when their nervous system is tightening, their tone is changing, their energy is leaking, and to course-correct in real time.

At its core, behavioural intelligence is built on three essential capabilities:

1. **Recognising your default patterns** – knowing what you tend to do under stress, whether that's controlling, avoiding, deflecting, or withdrawing

2. **Interrupting the autopilot** – having the awareness and capacity to pause long enough to choose a different action

3. **Aligning behaviour with values** – leading in a way that reflects who you say you are and the culture you're trying to build

Behavioural intelligence is what I call leadership in motion. It's not what you planned to say, but how you respond when the conversation doesn't go as planned. It's not what you intended to model, but what people feel after you leave the room. This is where real leadership lives – not in theory, but in tension.

Psychologist and author Dr Daniel Goleman, whose work on emotional intelligence has influenced leaders globally, puts it plainly: self-awareness, self-regulation, empathy, and social skill are better predictors of leadership effectiveness than IQ or technical skill (1998). In fact, in high-performing organisations, Goleman found that emotional competence was twice as important as cognitive ability in differentiating top-tier leaders from the rest.

This finding was reinforced in McKinsey & Company's 2023 global research, which revealed that leaders who intentionally model behaviour, rather than just talk about it, saw significant increases in psychological safety, engagement, and performance across their teams (Guggenberger et al).

In other words, how you show up matters more than what you know.

Self-management in leadership

Behavioural intelligence is also what allows leaders to lead themselves first, because leadership isn't just about guiding others – it's about managing your internal state so that your external behaviour is intentional.

Let's look at an example.

At a strategy off-site, a senior executive, let's call him Rob, was asked to facilitate a discussion about restructuring. It was a politically charged topic, and tensions were high. Rob came in with a clear agenda, but halfway through, a junior team member raised a concern Rob hadn't considered. The suggestion was valid, but it challenged Rob's plan. You could almost see his nervous system react. His face tightened and his voice sharpened. He cut the conversation short and moved on.

Later, in coaching, Rob admitted he didn't even remember getting defensive. 'I thought I handled that just fine,' he said. His team, though, experienced the moment differently. Several felt dismissed. One said privately, 'That's why we don't speak up in meetings.'

Rob's behaviour, though brief, sent a message. That message was louder than his entire strategy deck.

This is the subtle but powerful impact of behavioural intelligence. It's not about grand gestures but about micro-moments, subconscious signals, and the ripple effect of your energy, because your behaviour is your leadership. It's the real message people receive. Long after the slide deck is forgotten, what sticks is how they felt in your presence – whether they felt respected, dismissed, inspired, or invisible. Behaviour is what they'll remember. It becomes your brand, internally and externally.

We see this play out in every organisation. Two leaders might deliver the same message, but one leaves the team feeling energised and hopeful, while the other leaves them confused or cautious. Why? Because of the delivery, the tone, the body language, and the psychological context created by their presence.

What's critical is that behavioural intelligence isn't static. It's a learned, embodied practice like fitness. You don't just have it or not have it. You build it, stretch it, and strengthen it by paying attention, slowing down, and showing up more consciously each time.

It also requires emotional humility, which is the willingness to admit that what you meant may not be what was felt. That even if your logic was sound, your delivery might have missed. That just because your intentions were positive, the impact might still need repair.

This is the heart of behavioural intelligence: choosing responsibility over righteousness.

It matters more now than ever because we live in a time of leadership fatigue. Pressure is relentless. Teams are juggling uncertainty, burnout, hybrid environments, and rapid change. In these conditions, behaviour is a leadership differentiator.

In a 2025 study by Resume Now, while 86% of employees said their company communicates its values clearly, only 44% felt those values were consistently upheld by leadership behaviour (HRO Today). This values gap reveals that people are no longer tolerating leaders who say the right things but model something else. They are craving congruence, integrity, and alignment between word and deed. That's what behavioural intelligence delivers.

It doesn't guarantee that you'll always get it right, but it does guarantee that you'll know when you didn't and that you'll care enough to own it, repair it, and adjust. That kind of leadership builds trust, and trust builds results.

Behavioural intelligence is what turns your leadership from an idea into an experience. At the end of the day, teams don't follow titles. They follow consistency, emotional presence, and people who walk their talk, even when it's hard. That's the real driver of results.

Cultivating behavioural intelligence

Behavioural intelligence doesn't start with doing something different. It starts with seeing something differently. At its core, behavioural intelligence begins with one powerful and often uncomfortable discipline: self-awareness. Not the type of self-awareness that makes it onto your development plan. Not the polished, performance-review version where you nod through feedback and commit to working on your listening skills. The kind that makes you pause after a meeting and ask: 'Why did I feel the need to jump in and solve that?', 'What emotion was driving my reaction just now?', 'Was I really leading, or just protecting myself?'

This kind of self-awareness comes from turning inwards, from paying attention to how you actually showed up in the room, not how you hope you did. It's in that pause, the space between your behaviour and your intention, that behavioural intelligence begins to grow.

For years, I led multimillion-dollar negotiations in some of the most high-pressure industries: legal and construction. I prided myself on my composure, clarity, and ability to keep things moving forward. I knew how to win arguments and solve problems before they escalated.

What I didn't know, or what I couldn't see at the time, was how my need for perfection, quietly fuelled by a fear of failure, created a kind of tension in the teams I led. I thought I was being thorough, focused, and responsible, but my teams felt micromanaged. They second-guessed themselves. They hesitated to bring new ideas forward. Over time, they became more reactive, more guarded, and less creative. I wasn't doing it on purpose. In fact, I thought I was helping.

That's the hard truth about leadership: our behaviours are rarely malicious. They're often protective, learned, and automatic. They still land, though, and what lands becomes culture.

I came to this realisation during a long season of quiet reflection. After one particularly tense project review, someone on my team had the courage to tell me, 'We know you want the best, but sometimes, it's hard to breathe.'

That comment stayed with me. Not because it hurt, though it did, but because it cracked something open. It made me realise that I was shaping the culture around me with every email I sent, every comment I made, every sigh I let slip in a meeting. It wasn't my knowledge or my values that defined my leadership. It was my behaviour. That incident and a couple more situations I encountered made me realise things needed to shift.

When you begin cultivating behavioural intelligence, you stop obsessing over how to manage others, and you start learning how to lead yourself. In that shift, your influence becomes exponentially more powerful. The truth is that results don't happen because of pressure, control, or clever plans. They occur when a team feels psychologically safe. When your behaviour consistently signals trust. When people know that you're not just performing leadership but living it.

Leading through presence

We've seen it time and again: leaders who create impact because their presence allows others to bring their best. Leaders who choose to be intentional.

Take Amir, a regional operations leader I worked with during a major transformation project. On paper, he was a textbook high performer – KPI-driven, methodical, and relentless in his standards – but turnover in his division was quietly rising. Engagement was low, and innovation was stagnant.

During our sessions, Amir discovered that his behaviour under pressure – tight control, critical feedback, and emotional detachment – was the opposite of what he wanted to create: a culture of ownership, collaboration, and resilience.

He knew the theory, he could recite the mission, but his behaviour was telling a different story. It wasn't until he connected those dots, until he took radical responsibility for his own patterns, that things began to change. Not because he gave a big speech or rolled out a new team charter but because he started showing up differently: slower, warmer, more curious, and less reactive. Slowly, his team followed.

People mirror what they experience, and when a leader becomes more behaviourally intelligent, the ripple effects are visible in every corner of the culture. This is why behavioural intelligence matters more than any technical skill. It's what fuels trust, clarity, alignment, and psychological safety. It's what turns a collection of individuals into a team. It's the invisible infrastructure of every high-performing culture.

Thankfully, it's not reserved only for the select few. You don't have to be naturally charismatic or emotionally fluent. You just have to be willing to observe yourself honestly, to stay curious in discomfort, and to choose presence over performance, again and again.

Behavioural intelligence is the quiet choice to take a breath before reacting, notice your own defensiveness, choose curiosity instead, stay in a hard conversation without shutting down or taking over, and recognise the difference between having high standards and creating fear.

It doesn't always make a scene, but it always makes a difference. It's the difference between a team that obeys and a team that trusts. Between a leader who performs and a leader who transforms. Between results that are forced and results that are inspired.

Remember that leadership isn't about what you say you believe. It's about what your behaviour tells the room, especially when you're not trying to impress anyone.

Inspirational leaders

We often associate great leadership with bold decisions or powerful speeches. In reality, sustainable impact is rarely the result of pressure, control, or charisma alone. True leadership transformation comes from behavioural intelligence – consistent, conscious actions that align with one's values and desired impact.

The following are real-world leaders known for how they modelled behavioural intelligence in action. These individuals didn't just know what effective leadership looked like; they lived it. Their behaviours, more than their titles, created trust, momentum, and transformation.

Jacinda Ardern: Leading through empathy and emotional presence

As Prime Minister of New Zealand, Jacinda Ardern became globally recognised for her empathetic leadership style, especially in moments of crisis. After the 2019 Christchurch mosque attacks, she didn't simply issue a policy response or deliver a press release. She showed up physically, emotionally, and behaviourally.

Wearing a hijab, she embraced grieving families, listened quietly, and spoke with compassion. Her behaviour sent a clear message: this was not just political leadership; it was human leadership. That moment of presence united a nation, strengthened social trust, and earned her international respect. Ardern led through empathy, a hallmark of behavioural intelligence.

Satya Nadella: Shifting Microsoft's culture through humility and curiosity

When Satya Nadella took over as CEO of Microsoft in 2014, the company was known for internal competition and a deeply siloed culture. Instead of pushing harder or implementing stricter controls, Nadella introduced a behavioural shift rooted in a growth mindset, inspired by Carol Dweck's research.

He modelled vulnerability by openly admitting past cultural flaws. He encouraged leaders to stop trying to be know-it-alls and instead become learn-it-alls. Under Nadella, meetings changed. Leaders asked more questions, paused to listen, and acknowledged mistakes.

This shift from knowledge-hoarding to knowledge-sharing didn't happen because of a new strategy. It happened because Nadella modelled humility and curiosity. Microsoft's cultural revival and its resulting innovation boom can be traced back to intentional behavioural change at the top.

Barack Obama: Regulating emotion in the face of conflict

Barack Obama is known for his calm demeanour, especially under pressure. Behind that calm isn't just temperament; it is conscious regulation. During the 2009 healthcare reform debates, Obama was frequently criticised, challenged, and misrepresented.

He rarely reacted defensively. He often listened fully before responding. In interviews, aides shared that even behind closed doors, he didn't rush to judgement. Instead, he paused and reflected. He often re-entered high-stakes discussions with the same grounded tone.

That kind of emotional self-regulation is a critical expression of behavioural intelligence. Obama's ability to stay composed, without losing connection, earned him both political allies and public trust. His leadership impact was not just about his eloquence, but about the behaviours he repeated: calmness under fire, thoughtfulness in tension, and inclusion over reaction.

Angela Merkel: Practising deliberate, values-aligned leadership

As Germany's Chancellor for over sixteen years, Angela Merkel became known for her pragmatism, patience, and integrity. While other world leaders were often praised for charisma or bold theatrics, Merkel led through consistency and deliberation.

During the 2015 European refugee crisis, she made a decision that divided public opinion: opening Germany's borders to over one million refugees. Her reasoning was deeply values-driven. 'We can manage this,' she said.

Throughout her tenure, Merkel demonstrated behavioural steadiness. She rarely postured, avoided sensationalism, and didn't dominate conversations, but listened carefully and acted from principle. Her leadership legacy isn't marked by dramatic speeches, but by behaviour that quietly and consistently reinforced trust.

Oprah Winfrey: Leading with vulnerability and storytelling

Oprah Winfrey's leadership influence transcends industries. While she's not a politician or CEO in the traditional sense, her behavioural intelligence is what built an empire. She led with vulnerability long before it became fashionable.

Winfrey's interviews, even with global figures, were marked by active listening, emotional transparency, and deep empathy. She created psychological safety by behaving in a way that invited authenticity. Her storytelling, about childhood trauma, fear, and insecurity, gave millions permission to face their own. That behavioural modelling reshaped how media and leadership intersect.

Winfrey's influence came not from control or authority but from conscious, consistent behaviour aligned with her message.

EXERCISE: Five powerful questions to recognise behavioural intelligence

Before we close this chapter, pause and sit with these questions. They're here to invite deeper awareness, the kind that behavioural intelligence requires.

1. When you're under pressure, what behavioural pattern shows up most often? (Notice if you tend to withdraw, dominate, deflect, or push harder. Patterns reveal where your leadership is on autopilot.)

2. What impact do you consistently have on the emotional tone of the room, and how do you know? (Do people open up, shut down, become energised, or go quiet around you?)

3. When has your leadership had an unintended negative impact, and what behaviour drove that outcome? (This isn't about self-blame – it's about recognising the gap between intention and effect.)

4. Where are you performing leadership rather than living it? (Are there moments when you sound more aligned than you feel?)

5. How often do your behaviours reflect the leader you say you want to be? (Real leadership starts where your actions match your aspiration, even when no one's watching.)

Write down your reflections and return to them often.

Great leadership is shaped by how you behave. Every outcome you care about, every moment of trust, engagement, collaboration, and innovation, traces back to your consistent actions. If behaviour drives results, then the next question is: how do we become more aware of the behaviours we're leading with, and shift them in real time?

In the next chapters, I'll introduce the Shiftcode Model. This is a simple yet powerful framework to help you decode your leadership behaviours and navigate towards conscious, high-impact leadership.

THREE

The Four Pillars Of
A Thriving Workplace

What does it mean for a workplace to thrive? We often think of thriving in terms of performance: hitting targets, growing revenue, or getting ahead of the competition. High-performing doesn't always mean healthy, though. A truly thriving workplace is one where people feel safe, energised, and supported. Where collaboration feels natural, feedback flows freely, and trust isn't just preached but also practised.

In thriving workplaces, people do more than show up. They contribute with intention. They innovate because they feel safe to take risks. They care – not because they're told to, but because the environment invites it.

Culture is what makes that possible.

Workplace culture isn't built in workshops or decided in boardrooms. It's shaped in the day-to-day behaviours of leaders and teams: how people speak to each other, how conflict is handled, how feedback is delivered, and how values are lived when things get hard.

Culture directly impacts how your business is experienced by everyone you and your team interact with: clients, suppliers, vendors, and partners. The way your team treat each other is often reflected in how they treat others. A workplace where people are rushed, dismissed, or unsupported will eventually extend those same behaviours outwards.

According to the Society for Human Resource Management (2024), 83% of employees who rate their workplace culture as good or excellent say they are motivated to produce high-quality work, and executives are significantly more likely to rate their culture as good or excellent (82%) compared to individual contributors (47%). This 35-percentage-point gap reveals a critical disconnect between leadership's view and employee reality. Meanwhile, research from McKinsey & Company shows that organisations with healthy cultures outperform their peers by up to three times in terms of return to shareholders (2024).

In other words, more than being about employee experience, workplace culture is a business advantage. It's driven, every day, by behaviour. This is where the Shiftcode Model begins to matter, because we need leaders who translate values into action, who lead in a way that strengthens culture rather than erodes it.

Over the years of working across industries, from law firms to mediation rooms, construction sites to corporate offices, I've seen the same four qualities emerge in every high-stakes, high-impact environment. They are trust, engagement, collaboration, and inspiration.

There's a growing fatigue with performative leadership – leaders who speak about empathy but act from ego, who promise safety but model control. People are more perceptive than ever, and they don't follow language; they follow behaviour.

This chapter will introduce you to the four qualities – or pillars – necessary for a thriving workplace:

1. Trust

2. Engagement

3. Collaboration

4. Inspiration

We'll discuss how they function, what threatens them, and why behavioural leadership is the only way to truly sustain them. When these pillars are strong, the whole workplace rises with them. When they crack, the costs go far beyond the balance sheet.

Pillar 1: Trust

Walk into the meeting of a high-performing team, and you'll notice this quality within minutes. People speak freely, there's no second-guessing or posturing, feedback is direct but respectful, and decisions move quickly because there's no need to decode hidden agendas. That's trust in action.

Now walk into the meeting of a low-performing team. Conversations feel guarded, silence hangs heavy, ideas are withheld, and the meeting is filled with cautious language. People nod, but nothing moves. Everyone's playing defence. The difference is trust.

What is trust and why does it matter?

At its core, trust in the workplace is the confidence that others will act with integrity, reliability, accountability, and care, even when you're not looking. It's the knowledge that your manager won't use your vulnerability against you, that your colleague will follow through, and that your team will support you, not sabotage you.

Trust is a pattern. It's built through consistency, and in a leadership context, it's reinforced or eroded every time a leader chooses transparency over deflection, accountability over blame, and people over ego.

Patrick Lencioni, author of *The Five Dysfunctions of a Team*, identifies trust as the foundational element of all effective teamwork (2002). In his model, trust sits at the base of the pyramid – without it, teams cannot engage in productive conflict, commit to decisions, hold each other accountable, or focus on collective results. When trust is absent, Lencioni argues, teams become mired in politics and posturing, spending energy on managing perceptions rather than achieving outcomes. The workplace watching their backs and more energy creating forward momentum. They challenge each other in healthy ways, share ideas more freely, and bounce back faster from setbacks.

When trust is missing, energy gets redirected into risk management: emotional risk, reputational risk, and psychological risk. People start to play small, innovation dies quietly, and culture becomes transactional rather than transformational.

Research by *Harvard Business Review* continues to demonstrate that employees who work in high-trust organisations experience 74% less stress, 106% more energy at work, and 50% higher productivity than those in low-trust environments – findings that remain widely cited in current business literature (Zak, 2017). The original 2017 study's continued citation in recent years shows its enduring relevance and credibility. The link is clear: trust is a performance multiplier.

What trust looks like in teams

In teams where trust is strong, there's space for disagreement without fear. People speak up without scripting their sentences in their heads five times first. There's less need to manage optics, because people feel safe to focus on substance. In these teams, feedback is welcomed not feared; questions are encouraged not avoided; mistakes are treated as learning moments not as ammunition; people take initiative without waiting for permission, and leaders don't just talk about values, they live them.

In teams where trust is fragile, everything gets harder. Collaboration feels like a competition, meetings drag because no one wants to commit, people withhold concerns out of fear of retaliation or being labelled difficult, and projects slow down – not because of complexity, but because of emotional friction. You might still hit targets, but the cost to morale, engagement, and long-term retention is steep.

Trust accelerates everything

When trust is in place, everything else moves faster. Feedback is clearer, decision-making is quicker, and conflict gets resolved without emotional damage. In moments of challenge, tight deadlines, public setbacks, and unexpected change, teams with high trust pull together, not apart.

Trust doesn't remove conflict, but it transforms it from a threat into a tool. In trusted environments, conflict becomes about ideas, not identity. People feel safe to disagree, because they believe in each other's intentions.

Leaders who build trust become emotional anchors in uncertainty. Their teams know what to expect from them. Their presence lowers the collective anxiety in the room. That kind of leadership creates stability without the need to control every detail.

Trust as a multiplier of outcomes

In many ways, trust is invisible until it's missing. When it's present, it amplifies everything else. Teams with trust communicate more openly, adapt more quickly, and recover better from failure. They don't need to be micromanaged, because they're already aligned.

Trust multiplies four key areas: psychological safety because people feel emotionally protected, ownership because people feel their contributions matter, efficiency because less time is wasted navigating politics or clarifying intentions, and engagement because people feel seen and supported.

It also affects how your organisation is experienced externally. When trust exists inside the walls, it shows up in how your people treat customers, suppliers, vendors, and partners. External stakeholders sense it through tone, responsiveness, and consistency. They're more likely to engage with and recommend you, and stay loyal to you.

According to Edelman's 2022 Trust Barometer, we're witnessing a seismic shift in what matters most to employees. Trust has moved from being a nice-to-have cultural element to becoming the make-or-break factor in workplace relationships. In an era of widespread institutional distrust, employers who can build and maintain trust aren't just creating better cultures – they're creating competitive advantages that can't be replicated.

Pillar 2: Engagement

When people hear the word 'engagement' at work, it often conjures up images of mood surveys, pizza Fridays, or off-site team-building days, but genuine engagement runs much deeper than activities or events. It isn't about keeping employees entertained but about making them feel connected.

What is engagement and why does it matter?

At its core, employee engagement is the emotional and psychological connection someone feels towards their work, their team, and their organisation. It's about how they show up.

Engaged employees don't just complete tasks; they care about the outcome. They're more likely to go the extra mile, speak up with ideas, and step in when others are struggling. Disengaged employees? They do the minimum – not because they're lazy, but because they don't feel seen, valued, or connected to something meaningful.

Engagement is what turns a job into a contribution. When people are engaged, they don't need to be micromanaged – they manage themselves. When they're not, you feel it. Deadlines slip, enthusiasm disappears, and the energy in the room changes, even if no one says it out loud.

The business case for engagement

The link between engagement and business outcomes is no longer up for debate. According to Gallup's research, highly engaged teams show 23% higher profitability, 18% higher sales productivity, 10% higher customer loyalty, and 21% lower turnover (2025). Yet global employee engagement has declined to just 21% in 2024 – down from previous years. That means nearly four out of five people are going through the motions.

The cost of disengagement is staggering. Lost productivity, higher absenteeism, burnout, and a slow, silent erosion of team culture. Disengaged employees don't raise their hands. They don't challenge the status quo. They keep their heads down and their best ideas to themselves. The ripple effect is real: when one person disconnects, it affects the morale of everyone around them.

Why traditional engagement tactics don't work

In response, many organisations double down on engagement initiatives: anonymous surveys, social committees, wellness webinars, and themed dress-up days. While well-meaning, these efforts often miss the point. Because engagement isn't something you host but something you build.

Most corporate engagement efforts fail because they treat the symptoms, not the source. A Friday drink session doesn't make up for a lack of psychological safety. A team-building workshop doesn't repair the damage of a micromanaging leader. A mental health webinar doesn't erase chronic burnout caused by unrealistic expectations.

These are events, not environments, and engagement is not created in isolated events. It's created through everyday experiences: how people are treated, how they're heard, how their work is recognised, and how leadership shows up when it matters. You can't gamify your way into employee engagement. You have to behave your way into it.

Engagement as a cultural driver

When engagement is driven into the culture, everything shifts. People feel part of something, not just responsible for it. They move from passive compliance to active contribution. They trust that their input matters and that their leaders care.

In teams with strong engagement, collaboration is high because relationships matter; morale stays resilient because people feel connected to the mission; productivity increases not through pressure, but through purpose; and people take ownership because they see the bigger picture.

In disengaged environments, the opposite happens. Communication slows, friction increases, passive resistance builds, and culture becomes something that exists only on paper.

A study from the Corporate Leadership Council found that highly engaged employees are 87% less likely to leave their organisation than their less engaged peers (2004). More than a retention strategy, that's a culture strategy.

Leadership sets the tone

While engagement is co-created by teams and is everyone's responsibility, it's heavily influenced by leadership behaviour. Employees don't watch what

HR says; they watch what their managers do. They don't respond to slogans; they react to how feedback is handled, how recognition is given, and whether they feel respected in tough moments.

As one employee said in a recent coaching session, 'I don't need a ping-pong table. I want my manager to listen when I speak.' That's what real engagement looks like. It's built one behavioural choice at a time.

Pillar 3: Collaboration

We hear the word 'collaboration' in almost every organisation, tacked onto values statements, celebrated in strategy decks, or tossed into meeting agendas. What does it mean in practice?

Real collaboration is team members working in a way that brings out the best in each other, across roles, functions, and even conflicting viewpoints. It's about more than coordination. Collaboration requires trust, open communication, and a shared commitment to outcomes that benefit the whole.

What is collaboration and why does it matter?

At its core, collaboration within teams is the ability to engage with others in a way that feels safe, generative, and aligned. It means people are not just coexisting on a project; they're co-owning the process, the problem, and the commitment to success.

In a collaborative environment, ideas move freely. People lean into difference instead of avoiding it. Knowledge is shared, not hoarded. Responsibility is distributed, not deflected. Collaboration doesn't happen automatically, though. It's a skill set and a mindset. Most importantly, it's a behavioural practice.

Modern workplaces are built on complexity. Rarely does one team or one person hold all the answers. Whether you're navigating a client pitch, launching a product, or managing an organisational shift, success depends on how well people can work across silos, not just within them. That's where collaboration becomes a competitive advantage.

According to a 2023 report by Deloitte, organisations that promote a collaborative working culture are five times more likely to be high performing (2023). In cross-functional settings, collaboration directly improves execution speed, decision quality, and innovation outcomes.

It's not just about performance, however. Collaboration is also the bedrock of a healthy workplace culture. It creates a sense of shared ownership, builds psychological safety, allows diverse thinking to flourish, and holds a space for creative tension without personal fallout.

In high-collaboration environments, people speak up early. They resolve issues before they escalate. They bring problems to the surface, not to assign blame, but to move forward together. In contrast, low-collaboration cultures are slow, political, and emotionally expensive. People protect their turf, decisions are delayed, tensions simmer, issues escalate into conflict, and feedback becomes filtered through fear.

The impact of collaboration on teams

When collaboration is strong, decision-making is faster because information is shared, conflicts are resolved with less drama because people are willing to hear each other out, cross-functional projects succeed because alignment beats ego, and team morale increases because people feel they're building something together.

When collaboration is weak, even simple tasks become heavy lifts. Communication breaks down, meetings become battles, trust erodes, and talented individuals disengage due to the working dynamics. In today's hybrid environments, poor collaboration is costly.

Collaboration killers

There's no shortage of collaboration training in the corporate world, but most of it fails because it ignores the real blockers. These are the main things that get in the way:

- Collaboration dies in environments where **blame is the default**. When things go wrong, people look for someone to hold responsible rather than something to improve. Finger-pointing replaces feedback, and team members focus more on protecting their own roles than solving problems together.

- **Lack of accountability** is another major barrier. When no one truly owns outcomes, progress stalls, or, worse, people step back and let someone else take the fall.

- When **psychological safety is low**, people don't speak up. They won't challenge ideas, admit uncertainty, or take creative risks. In environments where mistakes are punished, the instinct is to play it safe, but when people fear getting it wrong, they often do nothing at all. That's when innovation dies and stagnation quietly takes its place.

Behind all these blockers is fear: fear of judgement, of being sidelined, and of being perceived as not knowing enough or doing enough. When fear drives behaviour, collaboration becomes transactional, not transformational.

This is where leadership behaviour becomes critical. Leaders set the tone; if a leader deflects blame, team members will too. If a leader owns mistakes and invites others in, collaboration becomes safer for everyone.

Collaboration isn't a bonus

There's often a misconception that collaboration is optional, something extra you do once the real work is done. In high-functioning teams, collaboration isn't an afterthought. It's a standard. Like any standard, it needs to be practised. That means:

- Giving others room to contribute, even when you think you know the answer

- Asking clarifying questions instead of making assumptions

- Listening to understand, not to win

- Taking responsibility for your part in shared outcomes

- Offering feedback in a way that builds, not breaks

Collaborative teams create cohesion through consistent behaviours that prioritise connection over control. When collaboration works, everything else works better.

Pillar 4: Inspiration

Inspiration isn't about motivational quotes or hyped-up speeches. It's not something you laminate and display on the wall. True workplace inspiration runs deeper. It's the sense of energy and possibility that lifts a room and leads to people feeling emotionally connected to what they're doing and who they're doing it with.

In a high-trust, psychologically safe environment, inspiration shows up in how someone chooses to care, speak up, solve problems, or support a colleague. When it's missing, even the most talented teams lose their spark.

What is inspiration and why does it matter?

Inspiration at work is the emotional lift that comes from purpose, alignment, and belief. It's the feeling that 'what I'm doing matters' and 'I want to give my best because this is worth it.'

Inspired teams move with energy. They connect ideas across functions. They anticipate needs because they're invested in each other. They rally when it's hard, and they recharge together when things slow down. They're connected enough to care.

In a time when burnout, disengagement, and emotional fatigue are at record highs, inspiration is a leadership responsibility. People are no longer just chasing promotions or pay checks. They're asking, 'Does this work matter?', 'Does anyone notice what I bring?', 'Is this environment worth my energy?'

If the answer is no, they don't necessarily quit; they just dial back. Disengagement happens silently. It doesn't always look like conflict. Sometimes it seems like compliance.

A global survey by McKinsey & Company in 2022 found that employees who described themselves as inspired were more than four times more engaged, twice as likely to stay, and performed significantly better than their uninspired peers (2022). That's not a small shift but a cultural multiplier.

Inspired teams versus compliant teams

There's a world of difference between teams who show up because they want to and those who show up because they have to. Compliant teams meet deadlines, complete tasks, and say the right things – but their hearts aren't in it. There's little stretch, little spark, and little shared momentum.

Inspired teams move with clarity and conviction. They take pride in their work. They care about the bigger picture, and they want each other to win. They challenge respectfully, contribute creatively, and, most of all, they feel alive in the work.

The most telling difference is that inspired teams don't just perform better, they feel better doing it.

The ripple effect of purpose-driven leadership

Inspiration is cultivated. It almost always traces back to one thing: leadership behaviour. Leaders set the emotional tone. When a leader operates from alignment, when their actions, tone, and presence reinforce clarity of purpose, people pick up on it.

Purpose-driven leadership is consistent, emotionally present, and anchored in real values. It gives people something to believe in as a daily, lived reality.

This doesn't mean leaders need to be charismatic or extroverted. Some of the most inspiring leaders are the quiet ones. They inspire not with volume, but with values; not with pep talks, but with presence. They hold steady when things shake. They model care under pressure, and that steadiness becomes contagious. The ripple effect among the team is more energy, more emotional safety, and more courage to speak up, take risks, and stretch into growth.

The influence of a leader

It's easy to forget that, in the rush of tasks and targets, your behaviour as a leader shapes the emotional experience of the people around you. The way you enter a room sets the tone, the way you respond to questions determines how safe people feel to ask them, and the way you speak about purpose, if you link it to real behaviour, gives your team permission to connect with it.

Your influence isn't just in the big decisions. It's in the small ones: every check-in, every meeting, every moment when your presence either inspires clarity or creates confusion.

People don't need perfection from their leaders. They need honesty, alignment, and consistency. They need to know you believe in the work and in them. When that belief is present, it shows. When it's absent, no amount of incentives can fill the gap.

EXERCISE: The behaviours behind your culture

Every workplace culture is shaped by repeated behaviours, especially the ones leaders model. Before moving on, take a few moments to sit with the questions below. They're designed not to point fingers but to shine a light, because behind every thriving team is a leader willing to reflect.

Use these questions as journal prompts, team reflections, or conversation starters. Growth begins here, in the quiet, honest space of noticing.

Trust

- What's one behaviour you tend to fall into that might quietly break trust, whether you realise it or not?

- What's one behaviour you consistently practise that helps others feel safe to rely on you?

Engagement

- What's one thing you do that sparks energy, ownership, or emotional connection in your team?
- What's one subtle habit that might unintentionally cause people to disconnect?

Collaboration

- How do you show up when collaboration is needed – what's one thing you do that helps it flow?
- When tension arises, what's one behaviour you lean on that could actually divide rather than unite?

Inspiration

- What's one way your behaviour inspires belief, creativity, or purpose in those around you?
- What's one recurring pattern that could quietly be draining morale, even if your intentions are good?

In a world where institutional trust is crumbling and employee disengagement costs the global economy billions, the question isn't whether workplace culture matters – it's whether leaders have the behavioural intelligence to build it. These chapters reveal the four non-negotiable pillars that separate thriving workplaces from those merely surviving: Trust, Engagement, Collaboration, and Inspiration.

These four pillars don't exist in isolation – they reinforce each other. Trust enables engagement, engagement fuels collaboration, and collaboration creates the conditions for inspiration. But here's the critical insight: none of these can be mandated, incentivised, or workshopped into existence. They can only be *behaved* into reality.

That's it for the four pillars of a thriving workplace. In the next chapter, we'll discuss what leadership excellence truly means with the Shiftcode Model and what it doesn't. You'll also see how the Shiftcode Model acts as a practical tool to uncover blind spots, elevate behavioural intelligence, and accelerate your leadership journey from the inside out.

PART TWO

THE SHIFTCODE MODEL: A PATHWAY TO LEADERSHIP EXCELLENCE

The path to leadership excellence is carved out through the consistent behaviours leaders model day in, day out, especially when no one's watching. If Part One uncovered the possibility gaps, the intent–impact disconnects, behavioural blind spots, and cultural erosion that quietly derail even the most well-meaning leaders, then Part Two is about building something better. This part introduces the practical blueprint for leadership that works: the Shiftcode Model.

Born out of real-world experience and deep reflection, the Shiftcode Model is not another leadership theory. It's a behavioural navigation system. A mirror, a map, and a practice. Whether you're leading a global team or influencing from within, this part will help you shift inwardly to show up powerfully outwardly. It's time to move from reacting to responding, from default to design, and from good intentions to lasting impact.

FOUR
The Shiftcode Model

The Shiftcode Model was created to do what many leadership tools don't: it translates abstract values into observable behaviours and gives leaders a way to see their patterns, understand their impact, and shift in real time.

The Shiftcode Model is built on two interconnected frameworks:

- The Shiftcode Quadrants

- The Shiftcode Compass

Each one is designed to do something different, but together they create a full picture of how leadership behaviours show up, how others experience them, and where there's room to grow.

Let's start with the Shiftcode Quadrants – the metaphors, because they're more than visual aids. They're behavioural mirrors.

The Shiftcode Quadrants: A behavioural map

The Shiftcode Quadrants reflect how your behaviour is showing up in the world; specifically, how others are experiencing your leadership. Each quadrant represents a leadership posture, a state of being shaped by behavioural tendencies. They are:

1. **Anchor:** Fear-based, limiting beliefs, biases, resistance to change – leading to stagnation

2. **Storm:** Reactive, controlling, or emotionally erratic leadership, driven by ego – leading to chaos, uncertainty, and conflict

3. **Sail:** Adaptability, curiosity, embracing change and challenges – leading to growth, opportunities, and innovation

4. **Lighthouse:** Intentional, values-aligned, and visionary leadership – leading to vision and purpose

These are not fixed identities but fluid behavioural zones that leaders move in and out of, sometimes within the same day. The Quadrants make the invisible visible. They show leaders the gap between their internal story and the external experience they create for others.

Why do these metaphors matter? Because behaviour is often hard to talk about. It's easy to say 'I care about the team,' but harder to face the fact that your presence feels distant or disempowering. The Quadrants and the Compass give leaders language. They create a non-judgemental, non-confrontational space to observe, reflect, and shift. In doing so, they build behavioural intelligence.

The Shiftcode Compass: A leader's internal GPS

The Shiftcode Compass reflects a leader's internal orientation: their behavioural direction under pressure, uncertainty, or conflict. It's a way to check in and ask yourself: 'Where am I operating from right now?', 'Am I reacting out of fear?', 'Am I aligned with my values?'

Like a compass in the wild, it doesn't tell you what to do; it helps you find your bearings. It guides leaders back to awareness, to resilience, to authenticity, and to intentionality, especially when things feel emotionally off course. In high-stakes moments, we don't rise to our ideals; we fall to our patterns. The Compass helps us catch that fall and redirects.

How the Shiftcode Model accelerates leadership excellence

Most leadership tools stop at awareness. The Shiftcode Model goes further. It helps leaders in the following three ways:

1. **Uncover behavioural blind spots:** You can't change what you can't see, and most leaders are too close to their habits to notice the ripple effects. The Shiftcode Model reveals patterns – subtle behaviours that erode trust, safety, or connection, even when intentions are good.

2. **Elevate behavioural intelligence:** This isn't about personality traits, but about choice. The Shiftcode Model helps leaders pause before reacting, reflect on how they're showing up, and shift towards behaviours that align with their values. It brings self-awareness and social awareness into the moment, where it matters most.

3. **Accelerate leadership excellence:** When applied consistently, the Shiftcode Model becomes a daily practice. It turns reflection into action, and good intentions into visible impact. Leaders begin to embody the kind of excellence that builds trust, inspires performance, and strengthens culture.

True leadership isn't about what you know; it's about what you choose in the moment when it counts.

Leadership is energy

We often think leadership lives in the things we say or the actions we take, but more often, it's felt in our presence. In the pauses between our words. In how we hold tension. In the unspoken signals we send in every room we walk into.

Your energy is your influence, even when you're silent. This is why internal shifts matter. Whatever we carry internally, stress, fear, doubt, alignment, or clarity, bleeds into how we lead. Our team responds not only to our instructions but also to our energy. That energy is contagious. If we're reactive, they shrink. If we're intentional, they are steady. If we lead with purpose, they rise.

One of the most important truths I've learned, sometimes the hard way, is this: *You can't expect what you don't embody*. You can't demand excellence from your team while modelling emotional volatility, inconsistency, or blame. You can't build a culture of trust while staying guarded or avoiding feedback.

Leadership excellence starts at the top, but it flows everywhere. This means that if you want excellence in your organisation, it begins with you.

Behaviour isn't neutral. It creates either safety or tension, momentum or mistrust, culture or confusion. The leaders who move teams forward are the ones who do the internal work consistently. They don't just shift others, they shift themselves first, and often.

Now that we've discussed the why behind the model, it's time to break down the how. We'll unpack the first half of the Shiftcode Model: the Shiftcode Quadrants. This is a map for understanding how your leadership shows up under pressure and how those behaviours impact the people around you.

This chapter is where things start to get practical, personal, and powerful. Come along with me.

The Anchor quadrant

This quadrant is when leadership is stuck in fear, limiting beliefs, resistance, and unconscious bias.

Let's say you're a leader trying to navigate change. The waters are choppy: tight deadlines, shifting priorities, and high expectations. You want to lead with confidence, but something's holding you back. You're not sinking, but you're not moving either. That's the energy of the Anchor quadrant.

The anchor metaphor is powerful for a reason. In the right moment, an anchor is useful – it grounds you and keeps you steady during chaos. Leadership isn't about staying in one place, though. It's about moving, learning, evolving, and adapting. When a leader stays anchored for too long, what once felt like stability becomes stagnation.

In this quadrant, leaders are often operating from fear: fear of failure, fear of change, or fear of being exposed. They're stuck in limiting beliefs: *This is how we've always done it. If I let go, it'll fall apart.* They're unknowingly guided by unconscious bias, favouring certain styles or voices while overlooking others.

What makes the Anchor quadrant tricky is that these behaviours often masquerade as strengths. Perfectionism looks like upholding high standards, control looks like being thorough, and resistance looks like having experience. Under the surface, however, these behaviours limit potential – not just for the leader, but for everyone around them.

The following are three illustrative scenarios showing how the Anchor quadrant manifests:

Scenario 1. The perfectionist senior manager

Melissa had spent eighteen years steadily climbing the corporate ladder in a national services firm. Known for her precision, polished reports, and relentless standards, she had recently earned a long-awaited promotion to senior manager and was now responsible for a high-stakes national programme with executive visibility and razor-thin margins for error. With the promotion, however, came paralysis.

Every document, from client proposals to internal memos, had to pass through her hands. Melissa would stay up late into the night, tweaking phrases, adjusting formatting, agonising over the smallest imperfections. A stray comma, a slightly misaligned bullet point, or a sentence that didn't sound strong enough could send her back to the drawing board.

At first, her team admired her attention to detail. 'She's thorough,' they said. Soon, though, admiration turned into quiet frustration. 'I feel like we're writing drafts just to be rewritten,' said Samuel, one of her most capable team members. 'It's like she doesn't trust us.'

Anchor behaviour

The truth is that Melissa wasn't trying to control; she was just trying to cope. Underneath her meticulousness was fear. A fear that one mistake could cost her everything, that she would be exposed as not ready, not capable, and not enough. She clung to control like a life raft, micromanaging every task until it suffocated the talent she had been promoted to lead.

Impact

As a result of Melissa's behaviour, deadlines slipped. Bottlenecks built up as everything was funnelled through her. Engagement dropped. Team members became disengaged, one even requesting a transfer. Innovation disappeared, as no one wanted to take creative risks under her scrutiny. Trust eroded. 'Why is everything taking so long?' executives began to ask.

Melissa's perfectionism, once seen as her strength, had become a self-imposed cage. What she couldn't see was that her team weren't waiting to be corrected. They were waiting to be trusted. They wanted to lead, to contribute, and to grow, but they couldn't spread their wings while she was holding them down. She wasn't leading a team. She was trying to protect her reputation. In doing so, she was breaking the very culture she hoped to build.

Scenario 2. The resistant operations lead

When his company announced the roll-out of a new digital workflow system, one designed to replace outdated spreadsheets and streamline manual processes, Kevin, the long-time operations lead, sat motionless in the back of the room, arms crossed, jaw set, and the kind of stillness that speaks volumes. 'This is going to create more problems than it solves,' he muttered to a colleague as the leadership team wrapped up the presentation.

On the surface, Kevin's reaction looked like defiance, but beneath it was something more familiar and more human: fear.

Kevin had been with the company for over twenty years. He'd seen trends come and go, weathered restructures, trained new hires, and built deep credibility through consistency, but digital transformation wasn't his language. The new platform felt like a foreign terrain. It was complex, unfamiliar, and quietly threatening. Instead of raising his hand and asking for support, Kevin chose the safer path. He resisted.

'We've been doing just fine with what we've got,' he'd tell his team, brushing off their questions with a reassuring smile that masked his anxiety.

When implementation began, Kevin silently undermined the change. He skipped training sessions, gave surface-level feedback, and failed to reinforce the system's importance in team meetings. His unspoken message was clear: *This isn't worth your time.*

Anchor behaviour

Kevin wasn't lazy and wasn't trying to be rebellious. He was simply afraid: afraid of not understanding, of losing the competence he'd built over decades, and of being exposed in a new world where his expertise no longer felt relevant.

Impact

His team, taking cues from his behaviour, disengaged. They didn't prioritise learning the new system. The change team hit a wall. Without Kevin's buy-in, momentum stalled. Efficiency gains were never realised. Other departments moved forward, but Kevin's team lagged. Silos hardened, trust fractured, and there were whispers of 'What's going on in Ops?' circulating.

By anchoring himself to the familiar and avoiding the vulnerability of not knowing, Kevin jeopardised trust, stalled growth, and unintentionally sent a message to his team: *It's not safe to stretch here.* What Kevin couldn't see was that his silence was shaping culture. His resistance wasn't neutral but contagious.

Scenario 3. The biased executive

Every quarter, the senior leadership team in Stuart's company gathered behind closed doors for succession planning. A long-tenured executive, Stuart had a significant influence on these discussions. He'd built his career on sharp instincts, fast decision-making, and what he often referred to as 'strong leadership presence'.

Over time, a pattern emerged. The same kinds of names kept rising to the top: confident, outspoken, and high-visibility men. Many bore a striking resemblance to Stuart in his earlier years. They knew how to own a room, speak with certainty, and project authority.

Then there was Diana. Soft-spoken but razor-sharp, Diana consistently exceeded targets. Her peers trusted her judgement. Her team thrived under her leadership.

She was deeply strategic, measured in her approach, and delivered high-impact results, but each time her name was raised, Stuart waved it off. 'She's solid, but I just don't see her commanding a room,' he'd say.

There was also Amir, an introverted analyst who had quietly developed a reporting tool that saved the company AU$300,000 annually. Stuart acknowledged the success but dismissed Amir as 'not quite leadership material'.

The pattern repeated itself. Those who mirrored Stuart's style – assertive, extroverted, traditionally executive – were championed. Those who led differently, often women, introverts, or culturally diverse leaders, were quietly sidelined.

Anchor behaviour

Stuart wasn't intentionally exclusionary, but his leadership lens was anchored in unconscious bias, shaped by decades of conditioning about what leadership should look like. His internal leadership blueprint hadn't evolved. It was narrow, outdated, and deeply rooted in familiarity.

Impact

High-performing, underrepresented leaders like Diana began to pull back. She stopped volunteering for stretch roles. Amir explored opportunities elsewhere, where innovation and quiet leadership were more visible and valued. Talented voices went unheard, creative potential stalled, and psychological safety diminished. Succession plans became echo chambers, lacking the diversity of thought, style, and background that modern leadership demands.

By anchoring leadership potential to a singular model of expression, Stuart was limiting the organisation's future. His bias wasn't loud; it was quiet, familiar, and invisible to him. To those excluded, however, it was deafening.

The common denominator

No one set out to fail, and no one wanted to disempower their teams, but behaviour, especially the kind rooted in fear or bias, doesn't need permission to have an impact. Anchored leadership is subtle. It hides behind experience, behind caution, behind habits that once served you well. In today's fast-moving, emotionally intelligent workplace, those same habits become the weight that holds everything back. Just like that, a well-meaning leader finds themselves stuck and unknowingly holding their team in place.

Recognising that you're in the Anchor quadrant is a good first step. Anchors aren't bad; they're just not meant to be permanent. They serve a purpose in moments of chaos, but when they become your default, they turn from protection to limitation. The key is knowing when to lift. The moment you notice your anchor is down? That's the moment you can choose to shift.

The Storm quadrant

This quadrant is a leadership metaphor for inner chaos.

Picture a storm at sea: thunder cracking, waves crashing, and winds howling in every direction. It's intense, unpredictable, and disorienting. Now imagine that same storm inside a leader. That is the Storm quadrant, where leadership is hijacked by reactivity, ego, and emotional turbulence. Like any real storm, it doesn't stay contained; it spreads fast.

In this quadrant, the chaos isn't just internal but also external. The Storm shows up in the moments when a leader is driven more by emotion than intention: snapping in meetings, withdrawing under pressure, and making impulsive decisions to protect the ego or avoid discomfort. It's the need to be right, to stay in control, and to be seen as certain, even when clarity is nowhere to be found.

Storm leadership feels loud even in silence. It's the clipped tone that shuts down dialogue, the defensive posture that makes feedback unsafe, the confusion that results when leaders say one thing but do another. It's a leadership style marked by mixed signals, emotional volatility, and unspoken tension.

The impact is swift and costly. Psychological safety collapses, trust erodes, teams retreat into silence or survival mode, productivity dips, collaboration fragments, and creativity dies in the shadow of unpredictability.

Storm leaders don't form in a vacuum. They gather strength from unresolved fears, unprocessed stress, and an unchecked ego. The longer these inner forces go unacknowledged, the more destructive the storm becomes. You can't outstrategise emotional chaos; you have to learn to regulate it.

Great leaders don't avoid storms but learn to lead from within themselves. They don't weaponise emotion; they notice it, name it, and regulate it. They stay grounded in the noise, create space for clarity, and when others are spiralling, they become the stillness that steadies the room.

Leadership isn't about controlling the weather but about mastering the climate within. Are you leading from the storm – reactive, scattered, or ego-led – or are you leading through it – present, composed, and steady at the centre?

The truth is that every leader has a storm. It's what we do with it that matters. Let's bring this to life with three workplace examples – anonymised stories from practice.

Scenario 1. The CEO who couldn't hear the truth – pillar most impacted: Trust

The boardroom was packed, but the air felt thin. A quarterly results meeting had just revealed that a long-awaited product launch had underperformed. The team was ready to unpack the lessons, but no one was ready for what came next.

James, the CEO, tossed his pen onto the table with a loud snap. 'This is a disaster. Whose fault is this?' His voice ricocheted off the glass walls like a warning siren. One by one, the leadership team tensed. A junior marketing lead tried to offer context about customer behaviour shifts. James cut her off mid-sentence. Another leader began outlining possible next steps. He rolled his eyes. 'We're not here for excuses,' he said. 'I want accountability, not analysis.'

In his mind, James believed he was demonstrating urgency and setting high standards. In reality, he was doing something else entirely: creating a climate of fear.

After the meeting, the corridors buzzed with whispers. A high-potential leader quietly started exploring new roles. A product manager delayed flagging a rising issue, afraid of becoming the next scapegoat. Behind closed doors, the executive coach who'd been asked to work with the team summarised the situation: 'People don't bring you the truth when they're afraid of your reaction.'

Storm behaviour

James wasn't a bad leader, but he was a reactive one. Under pressure, his emotions took the wheel: frustration became fury, disappointment became blame, and his need for control drowned out the voices that could have helped him most.

Impact

Trust shattered. Team members no longer felt psychologically safe to speak candidly. Engagement declined. People showed up to protect themselves, not to contribute. Collaboration collapsed. Feedback loops stalled, and leaders began withholding risks. Inspiration was absent. James's behaviour was demoralising.

Scenario 2. The email that broke the team – pillar most impacted: Collaboration

It was 11.34pm on a Thursday when the email hit inboxes. The subject line read: 'Disappointed and Done'. After a frustrating leadership meeting, Evelyn, the head of strategy, was venting her anger in an all-staff email. She'd meant to save the message in drafts and tone it down in the morning, but the sting of unmet expectations and missed deadlines burned too hot.

Instead, she wrote: 'Frankly, I'm shocked at the lack of ownership on this team. I feel like I'm dragging dead weight. If people can't operate at a senior level, maybe they shouldn't be here.'

By the time the team logged on the next morning, the damage was done. Some were angry, others were embarrassed, and a few were stunned. The email had been screenshotted, shared, and dissected across departments. A Slack group emerged, informally titled Walking on Eggshells.

The following Monday, silence reigned. Collaboration meetings turned into awkward check-ins. People stopped offering input. One team member started forwarding all decisions 'just to get sign-off'. Another removed herself from a project group, citing 'other priorities'.

Storm behaviour

Evelyn's email wasn't malicious; it was reactive: a raw emotional dump in a moment of pressure. In leadership, however, reactivity, even unintentional, can break psychological safety in seconds.

Impact

Trust eroded. Team members feared being publicly shamed. Engagement dampened. People reverted to doing the bare minimum to stay safe. Collaboration derailed. Psychological safety dissolved, and communication became transactional. Inspiration was lost. What had been a high-performing team turned quiet, hesitant, and fragmented.

Scenario 3. The COO who tried to inspire through fear – pillars most impacted: Engagement and inspiration

The town hall was meant to reinvigorate the company. Instead, it drained the room. On stage, David, the company's long-time COO, stood with hands clenched behind his back, scanning the 200 employees before him. The company was missing targets, and pressure from the board was mounting.

He began, 'What I'm seeing is complacency. There's not enough hunger. If you don't want to be here, no one is forcing you.'

His words, though polished, struck with the sharpness of a blade. A nervous laugh came from the back of the room. No one else moved. Afterwards, one employee turned to her colleague and whispered, 'I used to care. Now I try not to be seen.'

What David thought was motivational, like tough love and accountability, had landed as something else entirely: a message not of inspiration, but of fear.

Storm behaviour

David wasn't trying to be a bully; he was just panicking. Instead of creating alignment, he leaned into intensity. Instead of clarity, he amplified pressure. In doing so, he made people feel small when what they needed was support.

Impact

Trust cracked. People felt they couldn't show vulnerability without risking reprisal. Engagement withered. Discretionary effort faded, and so did initiative. Collaboration became compliance. No one dared to challenge or question the narrative. Inspiration extinguished. People didn't feel part of something; they felt policed.

The storm isn't you, but a temporary state

Storm behaviours, such as emotional outbursts, blame, sarcasm, and control, aren't signs of bad leadership. They're signals. Signals of unprocessed stress, performance pressure, or the ego trying to protect itself. The goal isn't to avoid storms. It's to learn to lead through them without becoming them.

When you lead from the Storm, you might get results. When you lead through it, you build trust, engagement, collaboration, and inspiration that lasts.

The good news is that you can shift. You can notice the signals, name the state, and choose a different way of showing up. You can be the calm inside the storm, not the storm your people are trying to survive.

The Sail quadrant

This quadrant is a symbol of forward-thinking leadership.

Imagine standing at the edge of an ocean, with waves swelling and wind rising, and the horizon wide open. Now picture a sailboat, not resisting the wind but adjusting to it, catching it just right. That's the metaphor of Sail leadership.

Sail leaders represent agility, curiosity, openness, and emotional intelligence in motion. They don't fight change; they harness it. They don't break under pressure; they adjust with grace. Sail-like leaders are not afraid of movement; they lean into it. They're coachable, curious, calm in the storm, and they listen deeply and lead with both clarity and compassion.

These leaders don't rely on brute force or rigid systems to drive performance. They lead from presence, adaptability, and shared direction. Their authority comes not from titles but from trust. They don't pretend to have all the answers, but they do ask better questions. They let their teams grow by modelling vulnerability, reflection, and feedback-seeking behaviours themselves.

If the Anchor keeps us stuck and the Storm breeds chaos, the Sail creates momentum that is steady, responsive, and values-aligned.

Let's see what that looks like in action.

Scenario 1. The manager who champions learning – pillar strengthened: Engagement

Maria had spent years in middle management, checking off KPIs and running well-oiled but uninspired teams in a large national health organisation. Then came the pandemic, and like many, she felt unmoored. In that stillness, Maria did something quietly radical: she enrolled in a short course on emotional intelligence. Not to add a credential to her résumé, but to better understand herself.

That one course flipped a switch. Through honest storytelling, she began integrating what she was learning into her team meetings. Every Monday, she shared one insight, sometimes from neuroscience, sometimes from a mistake she had made while parenting. She invited her team to do the same. Over time, that small gesture evolved into a cultural shift.

Maria created a learning wall, a virtual space where anyone could post what they were exploring. She encouraged team members to pursue short courses or listen to relevant podcasts. One analyst, Sarah, enrolled in a behavioural science course that led to a game-changing innovation in customer insights. Another team member, Jake, opened up about burnout and eventually led a session on boundaries and well-being.

What stood out most was Maria's transparency. When she took a misstep in a client email, she didn't hide. 'I got it wrong,' she said. 'I want to do better.' Her humility made growth safe again.

Impact

Psychological safety grew, as people stopped fearing mistakes. The team earned a reputation internally as the learning team. Retention spiked and innovation soared. Maria was promoted because she created space for everyone to learn.

Maria didn't push harder; she opened the sails, and her team caught the wind.

Scenario 2. The agile project lead – pillars strengthened: Collaboration and trust

Three months into a high-stakes digital transformation project, Arjun's team was behind schedule.

117

Vendors had gone silent, timelines had slipped, and the pressure was real and growing louder from above. Instead of panicking or placing blame, Arjun paused. He gathered the team – not for a reset and not for a crisis meeting. 'We're not going to pretend this is going well,' he said. 'But we're not going to spiral either. Let's recentre.'

He rearranged the chairs, brought out sticky notes, and invited every voice, regardless of title, into the conversation. They mapped out every obstacle, re-prioritised tasks, and reallocated roles. Arjun didn't assert control; he distributed leadership. He also took time to acknowledge small wins: 'That workaround saved us three days. Let's recognise that.'

Behind closed doors, he checked in on the emotional load. He saw the stress on one team member's face and asked gently, 'What do you need right now?' Arjun turned the storm into wind. The team began to move.

Impact

The project regained momentum, even if the original timeline shifted. Cross-functional trust deepened. Stakeholders began saying, 'That's the only team I trust right now.' The agile values weren't just written on the wall; they were lived.

Arjun's presence changed the atmosphere, and he wasn't trying to control the weather.

Scenario 3. The feedback-welcoming executive – pillar strengthened: Inspiration

Danielle had a reputation. She was sharp, strategic, effective, and also untouchable. Her team respected her, but they didn't feel her. They followed her lead, but few felt bold enough to offer her feedback or challenge the status quo.

Then came a culture pulse survey. It was neither scathing nor flattering. Words like 'rigid', 'out of touch', and 'disconnected' surfaced. Danielle didn't get defensive; she got curious. She started hosting informal 'listening sessions', with no slide decks and no pre-set agenda. Just real questions like: 'What's one policy that frustrates you?', 'What are we not seeing from your level?', and 'If you could wave a magic wand, what would you change?' Then… she actually listened.

When staff brought up the outdated parental leave policy, she said, 'Thank you. That never crossed my radar. But I see it now.' When junior employees suggested that career pathways lacked transparency, she made adjustments. Quietly, respectfully, and with follow-through. She even sent handwritten notes to those who raised the most uncomfortable truths.

At first, people doubted her sincerity, but when they saw their words become policies, scepticism turned to trust.

Impact

Engagement and innovation climbed. Inclusion became a lived value, rather than being a poster on a wall. Other leaders began to mimic her approach.

Danielle's leadership shifted from respected to revered. By opening her sails to feedback, she created a culture where people didn't just work harder, they showed up braver.

What makes the Sail quadrant powerful?

Sail leadership is powerful because it's present. Leaders in this quadrant:

- Don't fear feedback; they invite it
- Don't default to their egos; they model humility
- Don't wait for control; they move with clarity and collective input

That's what creates forward motion. In the workplace, Sail leaders strengthen all four pillars:

- Trust – through transparency and consistency
- Engagement – through shared growth and psychological safety
- Collaboration – through co-creation and open communication

- Inspiration – through humility, adaptability, and vision

While Anchors hold teams back and Storms stir confusion, Sails invite movement with adaptability.

The Lighthouse quadrant

In this quadrant, leaders guide with vision, purpose, presence, and principle.

Imagine a stormy night at sea where waves are crashing, winds are howling, and the sky is a curtain of chaos. Ships toss and turn in the swell, disoriented and desperate for direction. Then, cutting through the noise and the dark, there is a single and steady beam of light. Unwavering, steady, and clear. The lighthouse doesn't chase the storm. It stands still, and because it stands still, others find their way. That's the metaphor of Lighthouse leadership.

The Lighthouse leader doesn't have the loudest voice in the room. They're not the first to react or the one who charges ahead. They're the leader who embodies steadiness, whose presence brings clarity, whose decisions are grounded in values, not in ego, and whose light doesn't demand attention, but earns respect through consistency, calm, and courage.

Lighthouse leaders don't panic when the tide turns. They don't chase trends or react from fear. Instead, they return repeatedly to the grounding influence of purpose. They lead not to control others, but to guide them and light the way forward.

Their influence is felt most deeply in moments of uncertainty, when others are spinning, unsure, or overwhelmed. That's when the Lighthouse leader rises. They rise quietly, steadily, and reliably. They hold the emotional centre when storms brew. Because they are centred, others find their footing.

A Lighthouse leader is driven by principle. They make decisions that reflect not just what's popular, but what's right. Their strength comes from align-ment between values and voice, clarity and courage, and presence and purpose.

They ask themselves, 'What do I stand for when every-thing around me is shifting?', 'Am I casting light, or am I adding to the storm?', 'Can others collectively find direction in the way I lead?'

They shine not for recognition but so others can find their way. In a world full of noise, reaction, and over-whelm, we don't need more volume. We need more vision, leaders who are rooted not rushed, principled not performative, and who understand that influence is not in the spotlight but in the signal.

When everything feels uncertain, people don't look for perfection. They look for someone steady.

Someone who reminds them of who they are and where they're going.

Are you being swayed by the storm? Are you becoming the lighthouse your people need to see?

Now, let's see what that looks like in action.

Scenario 1. The middle manager who restored humanity to the workplace – pillar strengthened: Inspiration

Ravi had always been known for getting things done. As a delivery manager at a major facilities management firm, he ran one of the most demanding portfolios in the business: forty-two commercial sites, dozens of technicians, constant pressure, and almost no room for error.

For years, Ravi wore that pressure like a badge of honour. He prided himself on being unflappable, efficient, and results-focused, but something had shifted. The team that had used to crack jokes during toolbox talks now shuffled in silently and tiredly. Error reports were climbing, and sick leave that was had once been rare was now a regular fixture. It wasn't just physical illness; it was exhaustion, disengagement, and quiet quitting.

Ravi noticed, but for a while, he stayed the course. He doubled down on targets, ran tighter schedules, and held more briefings. Still, morale slipped. Then one morning, after getting off a tense call about missed KPIs, he glanced around the room and saw it clearly: this wasn't a performance issue, it was a people issue that no spreadsheet was going to fix.

That week, Ravi cancelled the usual performance huddle. Instead, he invited his team into the lunchroom. No projector and no agenda. Just a circle of chairs and a kettle on the boil. When everyone had settled, he said, 'I know we're running on empty. I see it. I feel it too. This isn't a check-in on work, it's a check-in on us. So I want to ask: how are you, really?'

At first, there was silence, then shrugs, and then, slowly, the dam broke. People started to speak, and, unsurprisingly, it was about burnout, missing family dinners, and waking up dreading another fourteen-hour shift. One technician shared that he hadn't taken a proper lunch break in three weeks. Another quietly admitted he was seeing a counsellor but hadn't told anyone for fear of seeming weak.

Ravi didn't talk over them. He didn't defend or deflect. He just listened... and fully. When the last voice became silent, he said, 'Thank you. I'm not here to fix you. But I will do better to support you.' At long last, he did.

Ravi added ten-minute well-being check-ins at the start of each weekly meeting, space for connection, and no KPIs. He advocated for flexible rostering with upper management, especially for technicians doing overnight callouts. He arranged for a mental health workshop as a practical, human response to the weight they were all carrying.

Slowly, things changed. The energy returned because the emotional climate got safer. People laughed again, and mistakes were addressed without blame. One tech, usually stoic, quietly thanked Ravi after a meeting and said, 'I actually look forward to coming in again.'

Impact

Absenteeism dropped by 38% in just three months. Client satisfaction rose sharply; tenants noticed the difference in technician engagement and responsiveness. Ravi was nominated for an internal leadership award. Not for hitting output targets, but for embodying values. For leading with presence, principle, and heart.

Ravi didn't rescue his team. He didn't pretend to have all the answers. He showed up calm, grounded, and human. He became the steady beam in the storm, a Lighthouse in action. As a result, his team started to rise.

Scenario 2. The values-led people leader – pillar strengthened: Trust

Monique built her reputation by never wavering from what she stood for. As a seasoned team leader in a construction and facilities company, she was now heading up a high-profile government project: a fit-out for a regional health clinic that needed to open in just six weeks. The deadlines were sharp, the political spotlight intense, and every delay carried a cost which was financial and reputational.

One morning, while doing her usual walk-through on site, something caught Monique's eye. A section of insulation had been hastily installed. It wasn't dangerous yet, but it wasn't right either. If left unchecked, it could compromise airflow, efficiency, and compliance. Fixing it meant tearing down part of a finished wall. It also meant losing precious time.

When she raised the concern with her project lead, the response was immediate: 'Let's monitor it. We're already cutting it close. No one's going to see inside that wall.'

Monique didn't argue. She nodded and walked away, but her gut clenched. She knew what that voice inside was telling her: *This is one of those moments that defines you*. That evening, she called her team together. She didn't yell or dramatise. She grounded the room in principle.

'We always say we lead with integrity,' she began. 'That means doing it right, even when no one's watching. Especially when no one's watching. Yes, this delay will cost us days. But cutting corners will cost us more. It will cost us our credibility, conscience, and trust in each other.'

Silence followed, then nods. Then, collective relief.

The next morning, Monique did what many leaders avoid: she called the client directly. She explained the issue clearly and took ownership without spin. She proposed a new handover timeline: four days later, fully compliant and structurally sound.

There was a long pause on the other end of the line. Then the client said, 'Thank you. That's the kind of honesty we wish more people had.'

Back on site, the team's morale, once tense and anxious, lifted. Jokes returned and focus sharpened. They worked with pride because they trusted that their leader wasn't just protecting the project. She was protecting their values. The ripple didn't stop there.

Impact

The client, impressed by Monique's transparency and steadiness, extended the company's contract to a second site. Her team's engagement and productivity surged. They didn't just meet the new deadline; they exceeded expectations. Monique was later promoted for modelling what trust and integrity look like under pressure.

Monique led with principle. She didn't rush to be right; she stood still in what was right. In the middle of complexity and competing demands, Monique became the Lighthouse. One that was steady, values-led, and quietly transformational. In her light, others remembered how powerful trust can be when it's protected at the moment it matters most.

Scenario 3. The CEO who brought purpose back to the business – pillar strengthened: Inspiration

The ballroom was packed wall to wall. Over 500 employees, from entry-level analysts to senior tech engineers, all gathered for the company's highly anticipated annual strategy address. Laptops were half open, coffee cups steamed, and conversations buzzed with a familiar tone of guarded expectation. Most assumed it would be another round of corporate jargon: revenue targets, market positioning, and a five-year forecast too distant to matter.

Then Leah, the CEO, stepped onto the stage. She didn't begin with a graph. Or a projection. Or a quote from a shareholder. She started with a story.

'There's a man named Thomas,' she said, her voice calm, steady. 'Last November, Thomas and his family lost everything in a house fire. Their home was reduced to rubble. He was left with nothing but a backpack and two terrified children.'

The room grew still. Leah continued. 'He filed a claim through our portal at 10.13am the next morning. Within six days, that claim was processed, approved, and paid because of a new back-end system our IT and claims teams had quietly implemented just months earlier.'

She paused, letting the weight of the moment settle. 'Because of that system, Thomas's children had a safe place to sleep that Friday night. Not next month, not after paperwork. That week.'

There was silence, then a few choked coughs, and a shift in posture across the room. Leah looked out at her people – not as a CEO commanding attention, but as a Lighthouse offering perspective.

'You didn't just hit a target,' she said. 'You gave someone their life back.' Then, and only then, did she begin the strategy presentation. This time, every metric pointed to a human. Every goal was anchored in service. Every department's objective was tied back to impact, not output.

Something shifted. In the breakout sessions that followed, teams that didn't speak across departments were suddenly swapping ideas. The customer support team approached the product team with insights, not complaints. Developers who usually tuned out the why behind projects started asking, 'How will this affect the customer experience?'

The mission wasn't just on a slide deck anymore but in the bloodstream.

Impact

Within three months, engagement scores across departments rose by 23%. Innovation proposals increased, particularly from frontline teams who now felt emotionally invested in the impact of their work. The company was featured in a national publication as a 'Purpose-Driven Enterprise to Watch'.

The real shift was felt in the hallways, where pride replaced burnout, and people showed up not just to do their job but to make a difference.

Leah hadn't just delivered a strategy. She had recentred the company in something bigger than performance. She reminded them all: *This isn't just business, this is personal.*

This is what Lighthouse leadership looks like. Leah raised the vision, and, in doing so, she reignited inspiration across every level of the company through clarity and heart.

Lighthouse leaders don't rush. They don't compete for attention or drown in drama. They remain present, principled, and purposeful, no matter how chaotic the conditions. Their consistency breeds trust, their clarity inspires action, and their calm becomes the compass others follow when the noise becomes too loud.

Whether it's Ravi creating space for people to breathe, Monique choosing values over speed, or Leah reminding a company of its mission, these are the leaders people remember because they stood still long enough for others to find their way.

Leadership as a state of being

Each quadrant of the Shiftcode Model reveals more than a leadership style. It shows a state of being. These patterns are not labels to wear, but paths to navigate. Whether you lead from the Anchor, the Storm, the Sail, or the Lighthouse, remember: none of these are permanent. They're not who you are, but how you've learned to lead. Once you become aware of them, you hold the power to shift them.

EXERCISE: Locate your leadership patterns

Before you can shift, you must be able to see.

The following mapping exercise will help you locate yourself within the four quadrants of the Shiftcode Model. You're not defining your leadership forever. You're simply noticing the patterns that have shaped how you lead and choosing where to shift towards next.

Step 1: Notice your defaults

Think about your recent leadership behaviours, especially in moments of pressure, uncertainty, or when things haven't gone to plan.

For each of the following questions, circle the behaviour(s) that feels most familiar.

When things go wrong, I tend to:

- Try to stay in control, do it myself, or avoid risk (Anchor)
- React emotionally, push harder, blame or defend (Storm)
- Stay calm, communicate clearly, adapt and adjust (Sail)
- Reflect, realign, and guide others with clarity and presence (Lighthouse)

When receiving feedback, I usually:

- Justify myself or avoid it entirely (Anchor)
- Get defensive or take it personally (Storm)
- Stay open and curious about it (Sail)
- Invite it regularly and use it to elevate others (Lighthouse)

In meetings or group dynamics, I tend to:

- Hold back or wait to speak until it feels safe (Anchor)
- Dominate, interrupt, or feel triggered by challenge (Storm)

- Listen deeply and look for connection (Sail)
- Facilitate with calm, clarity, and trust (Lighthouse)

When leading through change, I often:

- Stick with what's familiar or delay decisions (Anchor)
- Rush to fix, micromanage, or overwhelm others (Storm)
- Collaborate openly, communicate clearly, and adapt (Sail)
- Ground the team in purpose and lead with calm conviction (Lighthouse)

Step 2: Score your current state

Give yourself one point for each response under the corresponding quadrant and add up the points to create a total for each one.

Quadrant	Points
Anchor	
Storm	
Sail	
Lighthouse	
Total	

- Which quadrant are you leading from most consistently?
- Which one do you want to lean into more?

Step 3: Map your shift

Draw a circle and divide it into four quadrants:
Anchor, Storm, Sail, and Lighthouse.

Shiftcode Quadrants

Mark where you are now and mark where you want
to shift towards.

Use this as your visual tool. Keep it somewhere
visible as a reminder that patterns are not
permanent. You have the power to shift.

Step 4: Reflect and act

Use these prompts to identify the shift you're ready
to make:

- What's keeping you in your current quadrant?
- What behaviour or belief are you ready to release?
- What's one small, intentional shift you can practise this week?
- If you could shift just one behavioural pattern this month, what would it be, and how would it impact the way others experience your leadership?

Leadership is not a fixed identity but a state of being – a pattern of behaviours we repeat consciously or unconsciously until something interrupts it. The Shiftcode Model reveals four distinct behavioural states that every leader navigates: the Anchor, the Storm, the Sail, and the Lighthouse. These aren't labels to wear but paths to navigate, each representing not just a pattern but a choice.

In a world drowning in reactive leadership and performative management, we don't need more volume – we need more vision. We don't need leaders who are swayed by every storm; we need those who become the lighthouse their people desperately seek.

The Sail leaders show us how to move with grace and agility, catching the winds of change and turning them into forward momentum. They demonstrate that strength isn't about rigidity – it's about responsiveness. They prove that the most powerful leaders aren't those who resist the current but those who learn to dance with it, adjusting their sails while never losing sight of their destination.

But it's the Lighthouse leaders who remind us of leadership's highest calling. In moments when teams are tossed by uncertainty, when organisations are battered by crisis, when people are desperate for direction – these leaders rise. Not with noise or drama, but with the quiet power of presence. They don't demand attention; they earn respect through consistency, calm, and unwavering commitment to their principles.

Lighthouse leaders understand a profound truth: influence isn't found in the spotlight but in the signal. They shine not for recognition but so others can find their way. When everything feels uncertain, people don't look for perfection, they look for someone steady, someone who reminds them of who they are and where they're going.

The beauty of the Shiftcode Model is its fluidity. You are not permanently anchored to any quadrant. These are states of being, not life sentences. The moment you become aware of your patterns, you hold the power to shift them. You can choose to lift your anchor, calm your storm, adjust your sail, or become the lighthouse your team needs.

Leadership excellence isn't about avoiding the difficult quadrants, it's about recognising where you are and consciously choosing where you want to be. It's about understanding that every moment of pressure, every challenging conversation, every crisis is an opportunity to shift from reactive to responsive, from ego-driven to purpose-led, from creating chaos to providing clarity.

The question isn't whether you'll face storms in your leadership journey – you will. The question is, will you become the storm your people must survive, or will you become the lighthouse that guides them safely home?

Your team is watching. Your organisation is waiting. The choice to shift is yours.

The Shiftcode Compass, which is our next chapter, is your tool for doing just that. We'll discuss the four inner codes that make leadership excellence not just possible, but sustainable.

Turn the page and let the shift begin within.

FIVE
The Shiftcode Compass

You've learned what the Shiftcode Quadrants are. You've likely recognised yourself in more than one. Maybe you saw how fear keeps you stuck. Perhaps you've noticed reactivity showing up as urgency or frustration. Maybe you've glimpsed what it feels like to lead with grace and purpose, and how powerful leading from a position of being fully present is.

Recognition isn't the same as transformation, though. That's where the Shiftcode Compass comes in.

If the Quadrants reveal where you're leading from, the Compass helps you shift. It's a behavioural guidance system that takes you from blind spots and patterns repeated on autopilot towards behavioural intelligence, intentional presence, and authentic leadership.

The Compass consists of four core codes: awareness, resilience, authenticity, and intentionality. These are not abstract ideas. They are lived practices and inner disciplines that elevate your behaviour and redefine your impact. Together, they help you move from the fear-based behaviours of the Anchor quadrant and the reactive behaviours of the Storm quadrant into the responsive, conscious presence of the Sail and Lighthouse quadrants.

It all begins with the first and most foundational code: awareness.

Code 1: Awareness

Awareness is the ignition key of behavioural transformation. Without it, every other leadership tool remains theoretical. With it, you unlock the power to lead not by default, but by design.

At this point in your journey, you've already identified the patterns. You've begun to understand that leadership doesn't break down because people don't care. It breaks down because they can't see themselves clearly. They don't hear the tone that shuts down dialogue. They don't notice the clipped reply, the defensiveness, the subtle eye roll that sends the room into silence. They're unaware of how their stress leaks out and dampens collaboration, how their over-control chips away at trust, and how their avoidance erodes accountability.

The value of awareness

From the Anchor, unawareness shows up as micro-management, resisting change, avoidance, or perfectionism masquerading as professionalism. From the Storm, it shows up as emotional hijack, overreaction, intensity, or blame disguised as urgency. Both are forms of unconscious leadership. Both can sabotage performance, morale, and trust in ways the leader never intended.

Awareness is the moment you interrupt that spiral. It's when you realise this isn't leadership but survival, and it's not working.

This is why awareness is the first and most essential code of the Shiftcode Compass – because you can't lead others effectively until you learn to see yourself clearly.

Viktor Frankl, who survived the Nazi concentration camps, understood the power of choice in the most extreme circumstances. He wrote, 'Everything can be taken from a man but one thing: the last of the human freedoms – to choose one's attitude in any given set of circumstances' (1946). Awareness creates the space for that choice. It's not introspection for the sake of it, but behavioural intelligence in action. In today's fast-paced, emotionally complex workplaces, that intelligence is your competitive advantage.

The three dimensions of awareness

Most leaders confuse awareness with self-reflection, but awareness – the real awareness – extends far beyond the internal. It includes your ability to notice others and respond to context. It is multidimensional, made up of three interconnected forms: self-awareness, social awareness, and situational awareness. Together, they form the foundation of emotionally intelligent, behaviourally aligned leadership.

1. Self-awareness: See your inner operating system

Self-awareness is the ability to observe your thoughts, feelings, and behaviours in real time. It's not just noticing what you feel, but being curious about why. It's understanding how your emotions, biases, and stressors drive the way you show up. Research from psychologist Dr Daniel Goleman, author of *Emotional Intelligence*, shows that self-awareness is one of the key pillars of emotional intelligence and a strong predictor of leadership effectiveness (2004).

Self-awareness allows you to:

- Observe your thoughts and emotions without being hijacked by them
- Identify when your behaviour contradicts your values or intentions

- Recognise your automatic coping strategies, especially under stress

- Understand your impact, whether it matches your intent or not

Do you freeze when faced with conflict? Do you push harder when control slips away? Shut down when you feel unseen or disrespected? If the answer is yes, don't see these behaviours as flaws but as patterns. When unexamined, they become your reputation.

For example, you feel frustrated in a team meeting. Instead of exploding, you pause and reflect: 'Am I actually upset with them, or am I upset with myself?' This micro-moment of clarity can change everything.

💭 Reflection prompt

What emotion shows up most for you at work, and how does it shape your behaviour?

2. Social awareness: Tune into the experience of others

Social awareness is your capacity to sense the emotional realities of those around you, without judgement, without assumption. It's reading between the lines, recognising when someone's silence isn't disengagement but hesitation, and noticing when their defensiveness isn't resistance but fear. Leaders with high social awareness create psychological safety by making people feel seen, heard, and respected.

Socially unaware leaders talk over people, interrupt, dominate, assume, and unintentionally signal, *You don't matter here.* Socially aware leaders pause, listen, and inquire. They ask: 'What's happening beneath the surface and what does this moment need from me?'

For example, you notice a team member is unusually quiet. Instead of moving on, you ask gently, 'You've been quiet. Is there anything on your mind?' That invitation can shift the emotional climate of a team.

Reflection prompt

Who on your team might be struggling silently, and how can you create space for them?

3. Situational awareness: Read the room, respond with precision

Situational awareness is leadership agility – your ability to take the pulse of the moment and respond wisely. With this awareness, you know when to speak and when to stay silent. You recognise political undercurrents, and you understand when a tough conversation will land and when it will backfire. It's the wisdom of context, and without it, even the best intentions can backfire.

A situationally unaware leader walks into a tense meeting and charges ahead with the agenda.

A situationally aware leader senses resistance and says, 'Let's name what's in the room first.' This moment of tuning in can build credibility and connection.

☁ Reflection prompt

What emotional and political context are you stepping into, and how might you need to adapt?

The practice of awareness

Awareness makes you sharp. It's what separates good intentions from meaningful impact, turns silent conflict into open dialogue, and helps you shift, in real time, from reactive patterns to conscious leadership.

Awareness builds the foundation for the rest of the Shiftcode Compass. Without it, you lead on autopilot. With it, you lead by choice.

Micro-practice: The three-minute daily check-in

Start your day with this intentional reset and ask yourself the following three questions:

1. What am I feeling right now?

2. What might be driving it?

3. How do I want to show up today?

This simple practice rewires your awareness muscle and changes the tone of your entire day. Start with just one question each day to recognise your pattern.

Awareness is the first shift. It's a daily discipline that turns the fog of blind spots into the clarity of intentional response. You can't lead what you can't see, but when you do see and when you choose to see, your leadership begins to shift.

Code 2: Resilience

If awareness is the code that helps you see, then resilience is the code that enables you to stay: stay grounded, stay steady, and stay human without being emotionally hijacked.

Leadership isn't truly tested when the plan is clear, the team is aligned, and the pressure is low. It's tested in the heat of the moment – when something goes wrong, when the curveball hits, when feedback stings or timelines collapse. It's tested in those unpredictable, unscripted seconds between emotion and action. In those seconds, you will be triggered, you will feel disappointment, shame, fear, and frustration. What do you do next?

That moment, that choice, is where resilience begins.

Resilience is emotional agility

Modern leadership often confuses resilience with grit, endurance, or even detachment, but true resilience doesn't mean powering through at any cost. According to psychologist Dr Susan David, the author of *Emotional Agility,* resilience is the ability to 'be with your emotions with curiosity, compassion, and courage' (2016). This means facing difficult emotions with an open mind, kindness towards oneself, and the strength to move forward without avoidance.

Resilient leaders don't suppress what they feel; they process it. They don't pretend to be unaffected; they learn how to stay grounded even while feeling discomfort. Every time you react impulsively, like snapping at a colleague, shutting down, or overcontrolling, you reinforce the reactive patterns of the Storm or the Anchor. Every time you pause, process, and lead with steadiness, however, you shift towards the Sail or the Lighthouse; these are behaviours that cultivate trust, stability, and influence.

The cost of emotional reactivity

Emotional volatility is one of the most expensive behaviours in leadership. It costs clarity, credibility, and culture.

When leaders lash out, withdraw, or spiral into stress, it sends a signal, consciously or unconsciously, that the environment isn't safe, unpredictability is the norm, and pressure trumps people. When psychological safety erodes, performance follows.

Google's Project Aristotle, a comprehensive study of hundreds of teams within the organisation, found that psychological safety – when people feel safe to speak up, take risks, and be human – is the number one factor distinguishing high-performing teams from average ones (Duhigg, 2016). This groundbreaking finding validated Dr. Amy Edmondson's foundational research from Harvard University, which first introduced the concept of psychological safety and demonstrated its critical role in team learning and effectiveness (1999). The convergence of academic research and real-world corporate data makes a compelling case: when team members trust they won't be punished or humiliated for speaking up with ideas, questions, concerns, or mistakes, everything else – innovation, collaboration, and performance – follows. Safety isn't built in calm moments; it's tested in turbulent ones.

You can have the clearest strategy, the boldest vision, the sharpest skill set, but if your team can't trust your emotional presence under pressure, your impact is compromised. Resilience is what transforms leadership from reactive and unpredictable to composed and conscious.

Let's be clear: resilience isn't the absence of emotion. It's the capacity to process emotion without becoming it. To do that, leaders need tools. That's where the AURA technique comes in.

The AURA technique

The AURA technique is an acronym that stands for acknowledge, understand, reframe, and act. AURA is your behavioural reset button, a real-time method for moving from react to response, especially when your emotions threaten to hijack the moment.

Let's break it down.

Acknowledge: Name it to navigate it

You can't manage what you won't admit. Leadership requires not emotional perfection but emotional honesty. When we pretend we're not affected, we don't rise above the moment; we bury it. Eventually, buried emotion will leak out in your tone and energy, and in how others experience your leadership.

Psychiatrist Dr Daniel J Siegel calls this approach 'Name it to Tame it' (2011). The act of naming or labelling an emotion reduces its intensity and engages parts of the brain involved in regulation rather than just threat. Instead of telling yourself 'I'm fine,' try using one of the following responses:

- I notice I'm feeling anxious about this outcome.

- I notice defensiveness rising.

- I'm feeling overwhelmed and need a pause.

Acknowledging isn't weakness – it's leadership in action.

For example, you're in a stakeholder meeting. A colleague questions your approach in front of others. You feel the heat rise; the urge to cut them down flashes. In the Anchor, you'd shut down. In the Storm, you'd lash out, but here, you silently name it: *I'm feeling defensive right now*. That naming gives you back the wheel.

Reflection prompt

In what situations do you feel triggered, and how does your body respond before you even speak?

Understand: Get under the emotion

Your emotion is the smoke; the trigger is the flame. This step is about insight, about digging deeper to understand what that emotion is protecting or revealing.

Ask yourself:

- What belief or expectation is being challenged?

- What past experience is this echoing?

- Is this about now, or is something unresolved with me?

This is emotional intelligence in action. Leaders with high emotional intelligence have been shown to build more cohesive teams, handle conflict more effectively, and outperform their peers in decision-making. According to a study by TalentSmart (2009), EQ alone explains about 58% of job performance, and 90% of top performers score high in emotional intelligence.

For example, you feel angry after being excluded from a conversation about a project. Your immediate reaction is to withdraw. On reflection, you realise the emotion isn't about exclusion but about a deeper fear of not being valued. That insight changes how you move forward.

Reflection prompt

What is this emotion really about, and what need is it pointing you towards?

Reframe: Shift the lens, shift the impact

You don't experience reality. You experience your interpretation of it. Without reframing, you stay locked in the narrow story your ego is telling you. By reframing your perspective, you widen your lens and reclaim your leadership.

Ask yourself:

- What else could be true here?

- Is this a threat or an invitation?

- How might this moment help me grow?

For example, instead of saying 'They don't respect me,' reframe to 'Maybe they didn't realise how important this was to me, I can communicate that with clarity.'

This is what allows Sail and Lighthouse behaviours to emerge in a way that is responsive, not reactive.

💭 Reflection prompt

What meaning are you attaching to this moment, and is it serving your leadership?

Act: *respond with intention, not emotion*

This is the leadership moment – the choice you make next.

Ask yourself:

- What response aligns with the leader I'm committed to becoming?

- What behaviour right now would build trust instead of eroding it?

- How can I bring steadiness into the space?

For example, you feel disrespected. Instead of retreating or reacting, you say, 'I'd like to revisit that comment from earlier, it felt dismissive. Can we clarify?' That's emotional maturity in motion.

Reflection prompt

In a difficult moment this week, how did you respond, and what would alignment have looked like instead?

AURA in action: Your daily reset

AURA is a practice, a habit, and a muscle. Whether you use it before a tough conversation, in the middle of a heated exchange, or after a moment you wish you could redo, it builds behavioural strength.

Resilience is more than how you recover; it is how you lead when no one's clapping. It's staying conscious when it would be easier to collapse, pausing when your ego wants to prove, and returning to who you are, over and over again, until it becomes how you lead.

Resilient leaders don't suppress pressure. They metabolise it, regulate not just for themselves but for those around them, and create workplaces that feel steady, not stormy. With teams under constant pressure, the ability to lead from composure, not chaos, is no longer optional. This is the shift that separates managing from modelling, and it begins with one choice, one pause, and one breath at a time.

Micro-practice: The trigger journal

Each evening, reflect for five minutes by asking yourself:

- What triggered me today?
- How did I respond?
- What would I do differently using the AURA technique?

Over time, you'll notice the lag between emotion and reaction widening. In that space, your influence will deepen – not because you're perfect but because you're present. That's the gift of resilience, the power of the second code.

Code 3: Authenticity

Authenticity is about standing in your truth.

In a world full of perfectly crafted LinkedIn posts, curated leadership brands, and performative work-place slogans, authenticity is rare and powerful. It's the quiet force that earns trust, the invisible thread that ties intention to impact, and it's one of the first things your team senses about you, long before they read a strategy deck or hear your next vision statement.

Authenticity isn't about saying all the right things but about being someone others believe. No matter how competent you are, if your presence feels hollow, people won't follow you. They may comply, they may perform, but they won't commit. Leadership without commitment is just management in disguise.

That's why authenticity is the third code of the Shiftcode Compass. If awareness helps you see, and resilience helps you stay steady, then authenticity enables you to stay real. It's what transforms leadership from a polished performance into a living, breathing relationship, built on congruence between what you say, what you do, and who you are.

When that alignment breaks, trust erodes. As Dr Brené Brown reminds us, 'Clear is kind. Unclear is unkind' (2018). Being clear also requires courage – the courage to show up as yourself, not just the polished version; the courage to let go of performance and lead with presence; the courage to model truth over optics, alignment over image, and integrity over ego.

Authenticity is that courage in motion. In the Shiftcode Model, inauthenticity often shows up as behavioural incongruence. From the Storm quadrant, it looks like bravado, emotional dominance, or performative confidence masking deep insecurity. From the Anchor quadrant, it looks like passivity, avoidance, or silent resignation in the face of what needs to be said.

In both states, authenticity is lost because fear, pressure, and protection distort behaviour. The good news is that authenticity can be reclaimed. It starts with self-inquiry, with courage, and with daily behavioural integrity.

This code is about restoring alignment between your values, your voice, and your visibility. It's about leading from the inside out – not by performing a role, but by practising who you truly are.

The three practices of authentic leadership

Authenticity doesn't happen by accident. It's a daily decision to lead in alignment with your values, your voice, and your truth and to ensure integrity between your message and your modelling. That's what people trust and what they remember.

Here are three leadership practices that help you build that trust by aligning more deeply with your values.

1. Know your values: Live them out loud

You can't lead authentically if you don't know what you stand for. Your team can't trust you if your values only appear in your presentations. Your values aren't something you display on a poster or a checkbox on your performance review; they are your leadership GPS.

They guide:

- What you say yes to and what you say no to

- How you give feedback and how you receive it

- How you show up when no one is watching

The disconnect often begins when we think values are what we say. In reality, values are what we model, especially under pressure.

From the Storm, a leader may claim to value respect, but interrupt, critique harshly, or dominate conversation when challenged. From the Anchor, a leader may say they value growth but resist change, avoid hard conversations, or fail to address underperformance because it feels 'safer' to stay silent.

In both cases, the message and the modelling don't match. Over time, the team senses the gap, and trust erodes.

For example, you say you value inclusion, but do the same two voices always dominate the discussion in your meetings? You say well-being is important, but do you reward overwork with recognition while subtly ignoring those who set boundaries? The shift begins with brutal honesty.

Reflection prompt

What are the top three values you believe in as a leader, and where are your behaviours not reflecting them?

Don't just talk about your values. Make them visible in how you make decisions, hold space, and respond when it's inconvenient. Leadership alignment means people can predict your behaviour because it's consistent with your beliefs.

2. Drop the mask: Lead with transparency, not perfection

Authenticity is not the same as vulnerability dumping or unfiltered transparency. It's about showing up with truth over performance, presence over perfection.

Many leaders, especially those in high-stakes environments, feel pressure to appear confident, composed, and in control at all times. The paradox is that the more you perform strength, the less others feel safe to be real around you, and the more you hide your mistakes, the more people fear failure.

Leaders in the Storm quadrant often mask their insecurities with intensity, projecting certainty while avoiding emotional exposure. Leaders in the Anchor quadrant hide behind staying silent, avoiding risk, and pretending everything is fine when it's not.

Authentic leadership is about saying things like:

- That didn't land the way I intended, and I want to repair it.

- I'm not sure yet, but I'm committed to finding out.

- Here's what I'm working on as a leader right now.

This kind of honesty strengthens your authority. It creates emotional permission. When you lead with realness, others don't just respect you, they relate to you. That's what unlocks psychological safety.

In a 2022 *Harvard Business Review* article, Janice Omakeke highlights that leaders who demonstrate authenticity and vulnerability experience higher team trust and engagement levels, because people are biologically wired to follow leaders who show emotional consistency over perfectionism.

Reflection prompts

Where in your leadership are you curating an image instead of revealing the truth?

What would it look like to show up just 5% more honestly this week?

3. Model the behaviour you expect

Workplace culture is created not from what you say, but from what you tolerate. It's shaped most by what you model, not by what you mandate. This is where authenticity becomes visible through your leadership integrity.

Ask yourself:

- Do I ask for feedback but shut down when receiving it?

- Do I expect ownership but micromanage under pressure?

- Do I call for transparency but avoid difficult conversations myself?

Storm leaders demand performance but model reactivity. Anchor leaders preach accountability but default to avoidance. Authentic leaders do something different: they go first. They model what they expect. They admit mistakes. They set boundaries and honour others' boundaries too. They show emotional range, not emotional perfection.

For example, if you want psychological safety, be the first to say, 'I didn't handle that well.' If you want ownership, stop rescuing your team from discomfort. Your behaviour becomes the benchmark others calibrate themselves against. The higher your alignment, the more permission others feel to show up authentically.

💭 Reflection prompt

What's one behaviour you expect from your team that you're not consistently modelling yourself?

There's a common myth in leadership that authenticity is a soft trait – that being real means being emotional and that showing up with transparency means lowering your guard. Here's what authentic leadership actually demands:

- The courage to be consistent in a world of contradiction

- The discipline to act with integrity, even when no one's watching

- The emotional maturity to be seen – not as perfect, but as honest, human, and aligned

Authenticity is not the easiest path, but it's the most trustworthy one. It's the shift from performance to presence, from posturing to purpose, and from managing perception to modelling permission. When your team sees you stand in your truth, especially when it's inconvenient or makes you vulnerable, they trust you more. They believe in your leadership not because you always get it right, but because you're real.

This is how you shift from surface-level compliance to deep connection. This is how you shift from charisma to congruence. Authenticity asks for alignment, and alignment is what earns loyalty and trust and creates long-term impact.

Micro-practice: The 5% truth

Small truth, big shift. Each week, choose one space, one relationship, one meeting, one moment, and practise this question: what's the 5% more honest version of how you could show up right now?

It might sound like:

- I'm not clear yet, but I want to co-create a solution.

- That decision didn't land well, and I own my part.

- I'm excited about this direction, but also feeling a bit stretched.

Every time you show up 5% more real, you expand your leadership capacity, you widen the space for psychological safety, you lay one more brick in a culture of trust, and, over time, those 5% shifts become your signature.

You're no longer just managing, you're modelling. You're no longer just performing leadership but becoming the leader people choose to follow because you lead with your whole self.

Code 4: Intentionality

If awareness is what helps you see, if resilience is what helps you stay steady, and if authenticity is what helps you stay real, then intentionality is what gives it all direction.

This final code of the Shiftcode Compass is the integrating force – what ties your insight, steadiness, and alignment into a visible, influential impact. It's what transforms self-awareness into situational wisdom. It's what shifts presence into purpose and what turns behaviour into legacy.

You can be emotionally aware, personally grounded, and value-aligned, but if your actions don't channel those strengths into something meaningful, your leadership becomes self-contained. Leadership that stays inwardly focused isn't leadership but emotional maintenance.

Intentionality is purpose in motion. It's the conscious choice to show up – for yourself and for others.

The cost of autopilot leadership

Without intentionality, leaders slide into default. They operate from unconscious rhythms, inherited habits, and surface-level busyness.

From the Anchor, this shows up as playing it safe, avoiding the unknown, or letting fear of failure override meaningful risk. From the Storm, it appears as unchecked urgency, pressure-fuelled decisions, or a fixation on control that erodes clarity and calm. In both cases, the result is the same: people perform, but don't grow. Tasks get done, but culture weakens. Results are met, but relationships are frayed.

Intentionality interrupts that cycle. It pulls you out of survival mode and into strategic presence.

Intentionality in action: Show the way

Intentionality entails anchoring your leadership to clarity so that even in chaos, you remain a consistent point of reference. It begins with one daily question: 'What kind of leader do I want to be right here, right now?'

When you lead with intention, you move differently. As well as leading tasks, you lead the tone. You lead an emotional culture. You lead what others begin to believe about themselves. That kind of leadership outlives the project. It becomes part of who people are.

This code invites a simple but radical shift. Instead of asking 'What do I need to do today?' ask 'Who do I want to be while doing it?' It changes everything.

You stop reacting to pressure and start directing energy. You stop managing behaviours and start modelling beliefs. You stop demanding excellence and start drawing it out of people through presence and clarity.

Vision is a standard of intentionality. We often treat vision as something aspirational, a paragraph on a poster, a tagline in a deck – but real vision isn't what you say. It's how you behave when things get hard.

Your vision lives in the way you respond to tension, in the energy you bring into the room, and in the way you reinforce the standard, especially when no one's watching. Vision, at its best, is a lived experience: how people feel in your presence, how teams behave when you're not in the room, and how teams grow because you chose to lead with purpose.

The Lighthouse quadrant is the behavioural embodiment of intentional leadership. Lighthouse leaders don't react to the waves and don't panic in the storm. They stand clear and consistent and are purpose-driven so that others can find their way.

When you lead with intentionality, you guide transformation. People begin to lead themselves better because you modelled what clarity and courage look like. Intentionality isn't about being the loudest voice in the room. It's about being the clearest presence.

Aligning impact with intention

The intention you carry matters, but only when it lands. Many leaders have good intent. They want to inspire, encourage, or lead with empathy.

From the Storm, that intent is often distorted, expressed as urgency, abruptness, or control. From the Anchor, it's muted, buried under silence, vagueness, or avoidance. Intentional leaders take responsibility not just for what they meant, but for what others received.

They ask themselves:

- Did my tone match my message?

- Did my presence create safety or pressure?

- Did I show up in a way that moved people forward or left them managing my energy?

This is where the real shift happens: from unconscious leadership to behavioural mastery.

Integrated leadership: When all four codes come alive

When you lead with awareness, you become a mirror. When you lead with resilience, you become a stabiliser. When you lead with authenticity, you become a truth-teller. When you lead with intentionality, you become a compass. When you lead with all four of these codes, more than being present, you're directional. More than being connected, you're catalytic.

This is the shift that moves you from managing outputs to activating outcomes and from holding a role to shaping a culture.

> **Reflection prompt**
> Are your daily behaviours aligned with the leader you say you want to be, or are you leading by habit and not by design?

Whether you speak or stay silent, react or reflect, rush or realign, every choice broadcasts a signal. Intentionality ensures that your signal is clear, that your leadership behaviour is reflective of who you are and what you want to build.

You don't just lead processes; you lead people, lead energy, and lead belief – so lead with intention and integrity and like it matters, because it does. These four codes move leadership from default to design, and from influence to legacy.

Micro-practice: The intention-alignment-commitment (IAC) reset

This sixty-second daily practice anchors your leadership in intention. Ask yourself:

- Who do I want to be in this moment? (Intention)

- What behaviour reflects that? (Alignment)

- What one action will make that real? (Commitment)

This is a moment-to-moment choice. Every time you reset with IAC, you recalibrate your presence, and that presence is what shifts cultures, inspires loyalty, and builds legacy.

The Shiftcode Manifesto

Your leadership legacy begins with your next behaviour.

You've journeyed through the four internal codes of the Shiftcode Compass. Each one offers value on its own, but together, they form something greater: your behavioural operating system for leadership in today's world.

It shifts you:

- From autopilot to conscious choice

- From reactivity to grounded response

- From surface-level success to deep alignment

- From noise to clarity, and from motion to meaningful impact

With every choice, these codes move you from the Anchor and the Storm into the Sail and the Lighthouse – states of leadership that are clear, steady, and values-driven. This is behavioural leadership – honest, human, and intentional.

The Compass is now in your hands. With it comes the invitation to lead differently. You are not here to manage chaos but to lead through it and model the kind of leadership that transforms relationships as well as results.

Real leadership isn't about how loudly you speak but about how others grow in your presence. It is about daily choices that are built, practised, and refined in full view.

Let this not be the book you highlight and shelve; let it be the manual you lead with, in every meeting, every message, every decision. You are shaping culture, moment by moment. Choose the tone that builds trust, the pause that invites reflection, the posture that sparks engagement, and the behaviour that becomes your brand. Above all, choose to lead on purpose.

These codes don't change who you are. They return you to who you've always had the capacity to be: an emotionally intelligent, people-centred, and behaviourally consistent leader.

Insight alone doesn't create change, however, you have to live it.

Now that you've understood the Shiftcode Model and explored the Shiftcode Compass, it's time to translate insight into action. In the next chapter, we'll explore how to practise leadership excellence daily through small, consistent, behaviour-first shifts that create lasting impact.

PART THREE
THE SHIFT TO LEADERSHIP EXCELLENCE

Insight is powerful, but it's what you do with it that defines your leadership.

Part Three is where awareness turns into application. This is the moment you stop learning about leadership and start living it. The Shiftcode Model and the Shiftcode Compass have helped you locate where you lead from and what's guiding your decisions. Now it's time to practise the shift intentionally, consistently, and visibly.

Leadership excellence isn't achieved in theory. It's forged in behaviour and in how you show up, especially when it matters most.

Let's see what that looks like in action.

SIX

Behavioural Leadership In The Moments That Matter

This chapter marks a turning point. You've seen the Shiftcode Model and the Shiftcode Compass. Now the shift becomes personal. This is where awareness becomes behaviour, insight becomes identity, and the way you lead becomes felt and remembered.

Before we talk about mastering behavioural leadership, however, you need to be willing to see yourself clearly. When the pressure is on – when the project derails, the client escalates, or the team dynamics break down – that's when your behavioural quadrant reveals itself in your instincts.

The Quadrants in action

First, we'll be looking at an illustrative case study as a mirror. It follows four leaders navigating a high-stakes, high-pressure project, each operating from a different quadrant of the Shiftcode Model. Their behaviours shaped the entire emotional climate, disrupted or empowered collaboration, and influenced the project's trajectory.

This time, as you read, don't just observe the leaders. Place yourself in the story and ask: 'Which one do I resemble when I'm under pressure?' and 'What is my impact in the moments that matter most?'

CASE STUDY: The project that nearly sank – a tale of four leaders

A fast-paced facilities management company initiated a AU$10 million nationwide systems integration project. The goal was to centralise operations, increase efficiency, and modernise service delivery across all sites. With board-level oversight, a looming twelve-week timeline, and interdepartmental collaboration required, the project was high stakes and high visibility.

Four key leaders shaped the journey. Each brought something vital and costly, and each embodied a different behavioural quadrant of the Shiftcode Model. Let's meet them.

The Anchor: Olivia, senior delivery manager – drowning in perfectionism and control

Olivia had spent over fifteen years building a reputation as a dependable leader. She was the person you handed critical tasks to because she always delivered. In this project, however, what had once been a strength became a behavioural anchor.

Each day, Olivia arrived early and stayed late, red pen in hand. She reviewed documents that had already been reviewed. She held on to tasks rather than delegating them, because of her fears: fear of getting it wrong, fear of being exposed, and fear of losing control.

Olivia couldn't see that her need to be perfect was costing her progress.

Impact on the four pillars

- Trust withered. Olivia's team stopped offering ideas; they knew they'd be overridden.
- Engagement faded. Her team began disengaging emotionally and mentally.
- Collaboration broke down. Tasks bottlenecked at Olivia's desk.
- Inspiration was absent. The atmosphere was tense, exacting, and devoid of creativity. Her perfectionism was paralysis.

The Storm: Daniel, head of technical services – reactivity and ego over reason

Daniel was the firebrand – fast-talking, brilliant, and always 'on'. Under stress, his energy tipped into reactivity. When systems stalled, or contractors fell behind, his default was confrontation.

Meetings became blame sessions, voices were raised, and feedback was deflected or dismissed. To disagree with Daniel felt like a personal risk.

Impact on the four pillars

- Trust shattered. Team members filtered what they said or stopped speaking up altogether.
- Engagement diminished. Initiative vanished as people focused on self-preservation.
- Collaboration collapsed. Cross-team support faded, replaced by finger-pointing.
- Inspiration was suppressed. People delivered the minimum, not because they couldn't do more, but because it didn't feel safe to. Daniel's storm created emotional weather in which no one could work.

The Sail: Priya, project lead – adaptable, curious, and grounded

In chaos, Priya was the steady guide. She didn't pretend the problems didn't exist; she faced them. Instead of resisting reality, she worked with it. She pulled her team into collaborative problem-solving sessions, invited input, welcomed challenges, and adjusted with agility.

When a vendor dropped out, she reframed it as an opportunity to innovate. When conflict bubbled, she named it and made space to resolve it.

Impact on the four pillars

- Trust was strengthened. Her transparency created psychological safety.
- Engagement was elevated. Team members felt seen, heard, and valued.
- Collaboration grew. Barriers dissolved as people worked towards shared solutions.

- Inspiration was present. Priya's grounded energy encouraged ownership and creativity. Her leadership gave others permission to step into their own power and create impact alongside her.

The Lighthouse: Michael, general manager – purpose-driven, clear, and grounding

Michael was the quietest voice in the room but often the most impactful. He didn't issue mandates or micromanage timelines. Instead, he returned people to meaning, to mission, and to what mattered.

During the project's darkest week – when timelines were slipping and tempers flared – he didn't join the frenzy. He anchored the team. 'What do we need to realign?' he asked. Not 'Who's to blame?' but 'What's the opportunity to refocus and move forward?'

Michael modelled accountability when mistakes happened, upheld values when shortcuts were tempting, and reminded everyone of the human impact behind the technology.

Impact on the four pillars

- Trust was reinforced. He created steadiness amid uncertainty.
- Engagement was sustained. Teams knew they were part of something meaningful.
- Collaboration was elevated. Michael's influence connected departments through shared purpose.
- Inspiration was amplified. He reminded people not just of the what but of the why. Michael didn't just lead the team but lifted the culture.

💭 Reflection prompts

Where do you recognise yourself most clearly in this story, especially when you're under pressure?

Which behaviours in these leaders strengthened or weakened the four pillars?

When have you unintentionally mirrored Olivia or Daniel, and what was the cost?

What could leading more like Priya or Michael look like in your day-to-day leadership moments?

What kind of emotional climate are you creating: one driven by fear and compliance or one that fosters growth, trust, and ownership?

The table below shows the impact across the leadership quadrants.

	Trust	Engagement	Collaboration	Inspiration
Anchor	Eroded	Declined	Siloed	Absent
Storm	Broken	Fear-driven	Fragmented	Suppressed
Sail	Strengthened	Elevated	Solution-focused	Energised
Lighthouse	Reinforced	Sustained	Aligned	Uplifted

The story you've just read is a behavioural mirror. It reveals a universal leadership truth echoed by researchers like Dr Brené Brown and Dr Susan David: in high-pressure environments, it's not your technical skills that define your impact, it's your ability to stay emotionally present, self-aware, and behaviourally aligned.

Leadership is not truly tested in the moments you've rehearsed. It's revealed in the moments that blindside you when a meeting goes sideways, when tension simmers beneath the surface, when someone challenges your idea in public, and when your team needs direction but you're wrestling with self-doubt.

In those unscripted moments, your behavioural quadrant becomes visible. Do you freeze in fear? (Anchor) Do you explode in ego? (Storm) Do you stay open and adaptive? (Sail) Do you hold the vision with clarity and calm? (Lighthouse)

According to Dr Daniel Goleman, emotionally intelligent leadership is a set of learned behaviours, and behaviours are contagious (1995). Whether you realise it or not, your tone, body language, pace, and presence ripple outwards, shaping not just outcomes but team culture.

The first step is to locate yourself by looking at the four pillars of a thriving workplace.

Trust: Shifting communication through awareness

Trust is the invisible currency of every high-functioning team, and yet it's also the first thing to quietly erode when leaders lead on autopilot.

When trust erodes, performance may continue for a while, but energy drops, people protect themselves, communication becomes cautious, and innovation slows. What was once a thriving culture becomes transactional at best, and toxic at worst.

Edelman's Trust Barometer shows that 63% of employees say they trust their employer but that trust is deeply conditional. It's shaped not by strategy or salary but by everyday behaviours, especially under pressure.

Communication is the first clue – not just what you say but how you say it. Trust erodes when your words say 'I care,' but your tone says 'I'm too busy.' It fractures when your words say 'This is a safe space' but your reaction to feedback says otherwise.

Dr John Gottman's research on relationships, though based on personal dynamics, translates powerfully to the workplace. He found that trust isn't built through grand gestures but in sliding-door moments, micro-decisions, and pauses (2012). The way you respond when someone makes a bid for connection or truth is what makes or breaks psychological safety.

The most subtle missteps can send the wrong signal – like a leader sighing before responding to a question, an unread Slack message left sitting for days, or a skipped thank you or a failure to follow up.

From the Anchor quadrant, trust is weakened by hesitation, emotional distance, and the avoidance of honest conversations. The leader means well, but people interpret the lack of clarity as a lack of courage. From the Storm quadrant, trust is shattered by intensity, sarcasm, defensiveness, or bluntness that bruises rather than builds.

You may not say 'I don't trust you,' but the message is received through behaviour that indicates: *This isn't safe. You don't matter here. Play small.*

When people don't feel safe, they stop contributing, stop speaking up, and stop trusting you to lead them.

Real-time opportunity: A tense project update

You're in a team meeting. A junior employee, feeling hesitant but brave, raises a concern about risk in the project timeline. Your brain races because you hadn't anticipated this, and then the room tenses. You feel it: the urge to explain, dismiss, or power through.

This is the moment. Not next week's review or next quarter's all-hands – right now. Trust is either built or broken in this pause.

The shift: Awareness in action

Awareness is your internal dashboard. It helps you tune into not just what's happening but how you're showing up inside it. It's noticing how your tone just changed, how quickly you're speaking, and whether you're listening to understand or to respond.

Based on Dr Tasha Eurich's research on leadership self-awareness, most leaders believe they're building trust, but their teams experience them differently (2018).

Awareness gives you the power to shift. You pause. You breathe. You say: 'Thanks for raising that. If it's a risk, let's face it early. Can you walk us through what you're seeing?' That one moment of calm, receptive presence signals: *You're safe. You're heard. We solve things together.*

Trust begins again.

Practice: Daily trust-building communication audit

Before a conversation or meeting, ask yourself, 'What do I want them to feel?', 'Is this interaction about control or connection?'

In the moment, notice tone, body language, and pace. Are you grounding the room or escalating it?

Afterwards, ask yourself, 'Did my words and, more importantly, my energy build or break trust?' Ask your team and make feedback a two-way street.

Trust is built by how safe others feel to respond to your leadership. As Stephen Covey put it, 'You can't talk your way out of something you behaved your way into' (2012).

Reflection prompt

Where in your communication do you default to silence, control, or emotional reaction, and how could greater awareness shift you into leadership that earns trust?

Engagement: Leading through resilience in uncertainty

Engagement isn't about smiles in the hallway or enthusiasm in all-staff emails. True engagement is an emotional commitment. It's when people care deeply – not just about their tasks, but about the mission, the team, and the impact.

Emotional volatility from leaders creates instability. When leaders are unpredictable, vague, dismissive, or reactive, employees don't feel safe to care. Care requires vulnerability, and vulnerability doesn't survive in a climate of fear or indifference.

From the Storm quadrant, reactivity creates pressure that overwhelms. Teams start walking on eggshells. From the Anchor quadrant, emotional detachment leads to confusion and passivity. Teams tune out. In both cases, engagement dies quietly, one missed opportunity at a time.

Real-time opportunity: The unexpected curveball

In a monthly team check-in, a critical task is revealed to be behind schedule. The tension in the room thickens, and all eyes shift to you, the leader.

You feel the panic rise. Storm reaction: 'This isn't acceptable. Fix it.' Anchor reaction: 'Let's discuss this offline.' Neither response builds engagement.

The shift: Resilience in action

Resilience is not carrying on through gritted teeth or masking your emotions. It's returning to the centre, again and again.

In the previous chapter, we discussed how Harvard psychologist Dr Susan David called this emotional agility. It's the skill of recognising your inner experience without being ruled by it. It's the pause that prevents damage and preserves influence.

You breathe, ground yourself, and say: 'OK. That's not ideal, but it's important we understand what happened without blame. Let's unpack it and move forward together.' This way, you didn't collapse or explode. You created safety. In that space, engagement deepens.

Practice: The AURA reset

To help you in these moments, have a go at the AURA technique introduced earlier.

1. **A**cknowledge: I feel tension rising. That's OK.

2. **U**nderstand: What's this about for me? Pressure? Control?

3. **R**eframe: What would leading from steadiness look like right now?

4. **A**ct: How can I choose clarity over chaos and steadiness over sharpness?

Reflection prompts

When your team looks to you in moments of uncertainty, do they see stability or volatility?

What shift would you need to practise to become a leader who engages under pressure, not just in periods of calm?

Collaboration: Fostering safety through authenticity

Collaboration is a mood. It's not built in breakout rooms or brainstorming sessions. It's built in the emotional field of the team – whether people feel safe to be themselves, speak honestly, and offer dissent without fear of ridicule or repercussion.

Collaboration breaking down rarely begins with a blow-up. It starts in the small silences: the idea someone doesn't voice, the challenge they soften to avoid conflict, and the half-truth they share, sensing that full honesty isn't welcome. These are not strategy problems but safety problems.

Psychological safety – the belief that you won't be punished for making a mistake or showing vulnerability – is the cornerstone of meaningful collaboration. Dr Amy Edmondson's research on team effectiveness (1999) and Google's Project Aristotle (Duhigg, 2016) both confirmed this, showing that psychological safety consistently ranks as the most critical factor in high-performing teams.

Psychological safety is, however, fragile. It lives in behaviours, especially that of leaders.

From the Anchor quadrant, leaders create quiet tension by avoiding discomfort. They play it safe, side-step the tough calls, and disengage when things get messy. Their team mirrors this tension by contributing only surface-level insights, staying agreeable, and holding back their full perspectives.

From the Storm quadrant, collaboration breaks down in the noise. Leaders interrupt, push their agendas, or use force instead of curiosity. The message is usually, *We're not actually collaborating. We're complying.* When people don't feel they can be real, they stop showing up fully.

Real-time opportunity: A risky idea in the room

You're in a planning session. A team member offers a bold, unconventional idea. Before you can stop yourself, your brain kicks in and you say: 'That won't work. We tried something similar two years ago, so it's too risky.' You feel the impulse rise to dismiss, to redirect, and to get back on track.

From the Storm, you cut it off: 'We've done this. Didn't work.' From the Anchor, you nod vaguely and move on, and the idea quietly dies. In both cases, a message is sent: *Play it safe. Don't challenge, don't be weird, and don't be bold.*

The shift: Authenticity in action

Authentic leadership entails modelling the courage to explore what's real by saying: 'That's an unexpected angle, and I appreciate you putting it forward. Let's check it' or 'Honestly? Part of me feels unsure. But maybe that's exactly why we should talk about it.'

This is what Dr Brené Brown calls rumbling with vulnerability – leaning into discomfort with curiosity and courage (2019). When you do that, you stop performing strength and start practising it. You signal: *This is a place where truth is welcome,* allowing the team to lean in.

Practice: From mask to mirror

The next time you catch yourself defaulting to the 'polished' version of yourself, try shifting from *mask to mirror.*

Say something that reflects what's actually true inside you, such as:

- I'm carrying some tension into this meeting, and I want to acknowledge it.
- This may not be fully formed, but here's what I'm thinking.

When leaders mirror their real experience instead of masking it, teams mirror that honesty back – and safety deepens.

Authenticity is congruence. When your values, your presence, your tone, and your words all reflect the same truth, you create emotional safety without saying a word.

Reflection prompts

Where in your leadership are you over-curating, overcontrolling, or holding back the truth?

What would it look like to lead just a little more realistically and invite others to do the same?

Inspiration: Leading with intentionality when it counts

Inspiration is clarity. It's not about fireworks, focus, or how fired up you are in the team meeting. It's about what your presence awakens in others when things get hard.

Inspiration disappears when leadership becomes mechanical, when there's motion but no meaning, when goals are delivered but no one remembers why they matter, when execution happens but no one feels emotionally connected to the outcome.

From the Anchor quadrant, leaders avoid hard conversations or under-communicate purpose. They let the work speak for itself, not realising the team is quietly losing its grip. From the Storm quadrant, leaders crank the pressure higher, mistaking intensity for clarity. Urgency replaces purpose, and fear replaces belief. In both cases, people may continue working, but the light in their eyes fades.

That light is your culture.

Real-time opportunity: A fatigued team near the finish line

It's the end of a brutal quarter. The deliverable is nearly done, but morale is low. People are tired, frayed, and flat. You see it in the silence, slumped shoulders, and sighs.

From the Storm, you could push and say something like 'Let's just finish strong. I need this by Friday.' From the Anchor, you could say nothing and assume they remember the why.

The Lighthouse leader pauses and steps into intentionality: 'I know it's been a stretch, and I see what you've carried. This isn't just about hitting a deadline. It's about what we stand for as a team. The way we finish says something about who we are.'

Suddenly, the deliverable becomes a message, a moment of meaning, and energy shifts.

The shift: Intentionality in action

Every leader carries a vision, but it only becomes real when it shows up in action. Intentionality is that bridge – the conscious choice to align tone, behaviour, and presence so that leadership is not just what you say, but what others experience.

Practice: IAC

Have a go at the IAC reset introduced earlier:

1. **I**ntention: What emotional tone do I want to create right now?

2. **A**lignment: What behaviour would match that tone?

3. **C**ommitment: What small action can I take to anchor that intention?

This is how vision becomes visible, and leadership becomes art, not just output.

Inspiration is a consistent alignment between what you say, how you show up, and what others feel in your presence. As Simon Sinek reminds us: 'People don't buy what you do. They buy why you do it' (2009). Intentionality gives your why a heartbeat.

Reflection prompts

When people walk away from interactions with you, are they energised, focused, and connected to purpose or are they just executing the process?

What would leading with greater intentionality invite into the room?

Integrating the quadrants

Transformation happens in momentum.

Leadership transformation is a continuous and conscious practice, a recalibration of how you think, feel, respond, and influence others. Like all high-performance disciplines, the key to mastering it is reflection.

This weekly integration practice is designed to embed the Shiftcode Compass into your leadership rhythm. It's where insight meets accountability. It helps you track progress, notice patterns, and build the muscle of intentional behavioural leadership.

Integration practice 1: Weekly behavioural reflection

At the end of each week, create space to pause and look inwards – not to judge, but to learn, not to fix but to refocus. Follow these steps:

1. Capture the shift

2. Name the pattern

3. Choose the next shift

1. Capture the shift

What behaviour did you shift this week, however small? When did you show up as the leader you aspire to be?'

Maybe you paused before reacting in a high-pressure meeting. Perhaps you named an emotion instead of suppressing it, asked a better question, chose a calmer tone, or spoke with more purpose.

Document and celebrate it. These small shifts are proof that you're doing the work.

2. Name the pattern

Where did you default to the Anchor or Storm this week? Where did you compromise your values, and why?

Did you avoid a hard conversation, control a process, speak with edge instead of empathy, or rush through a meeting instead of listening?

Identifying where your behavioural autopilot took over is useful feedback. It reveals where your reflexes are stronger than your intention. Use it to course-correct, because awareness without reflection leads to repetition.

3. Choose the next shift

What quadrant do you want to lead from next week, and which code will help you get there? What's one conversation you need to approach differently next week?

Feeling stuck in the Anchor? Practise awareness. Losing people in the Storm? Strengthen resilience.

Hiding behind your role? Step into authenticity. Feeling reactive or scattered? Recommit to intentionality.

Choose to rise into either the Sail or the Lighthouse quadrant and choose one code to embody. Focus is what makes transformation practical. You don't need to shift everything; you just need to shift one thing on purpose.

You don't need to master every code, pillar, or quadrant overnight. When you practise one code, in one moment, in one conversation, you begin to lead with excellence. Leadership excellence, practised consistently, becomes your new identity, when you pause instead of react, listen instead of defend, and realign instead of retreat.

This is the work and the path.

Transformation is not sustained through awareness alone. It requires support, accountability, and a deeper commitment to integration in the real world, with real people, and with real pressure.

The Shiftcode Compass is your tool for that journey, but even the most accurate compass can't move you forward unless it's placed in the hands of someone willing to navigate with clarity, courage, and consistency.

If you're ready to sharpen your leadership edge, elevate your impact, and embed these codes into your team, your culture, and your identity as a leader, you don't need to do it alone, and you just need to take the next step.

For now, take what you've learned here and begin. Remember, the shift happens by choice. Every day, in every interaction, you have the opportunity to choose who you become. Lead wisely, lead deliberately, and lead on purpose.

By now, you've checked your leadership behaviours, mapped your default quadrant, and begun to embody the codes that drive excellence, but leadership transformation doesn't stop with you; it scales through others. Behavioural excellence is most powerful when it becomes collective.

In the next chapter, we'll discuss how to coach your team using the Shiftcode Model, turning your personal growth into a culture-shaping force. You'll learn how to hold space, build coaching capacity, and embed behavioural excellence into everyday leadership conversations.

SEVEN

From Personal Practice To Collective Excellence

You've done the internal work, reflected, realigned, and begun shifting your own behaviours through the codes of awareness, resilience, authenticity, and intentionality. True leadership excellence, however, doesn't end with personal transformation; it expands through collective impact.

This chapter is your invitation to coach your team towards behavioural excellence with the Shiftcode Model. Your leadership is measured not just by what you achieve but by what you activate in others. The greatest leaders are not just high performers – they're high multipliers. They don't just model excellence but build it in the people around them.

Leadership today is a relational, moment-by-moment practice of helping others see themselves clearly, shift consciously, and lead courageously. This is where coaching meets culture and where the Shiftcode Model becomes more than a personal lens; it becomes a shared leadership language.

As Harvard's Dr Robert Kegan notes in his work on adult development, 'Most people are living in a reactive mindset without realising it' (2013). The role of a leader is to create an environment where others can evolve out of that reactivity and into intentionality.' This chapter helps you do just that.

Let's discuss how to coach your team using the Shiftcode Model so that excellence lives not only in you but also in your people, your culture, and your collective success.

A coaching and mentoring framework

Whether you realise it or not, you are already coaching your team. Every feedback moment, every one-to-one, and every missed opportunity to pause or praise is sending a message. The question is: are you doing it consciously?

The Shiftcode Model allows you to move from reactive correction to intentional coaching. It equips you with a shared behavioural language that normalises feedback, builds trust, and makes growth safe. Instead of pointing fingers, you hold up a mirror. You shift from blame to behaviour and from personality to patterns.

For example, instead of saying 'You're being defensive again,' you ask 'Do you think we're in the Storm quadrant right now?'

This non-confrontational, depersonalised language reduces shame, encourages ownership, and makes self-awareness easier to access. Thankfully, the Shiftcode Model provides both clarity and compassion in behavioural feedback.

Step 1: Use the Quadrants to reflect, not diagnose

Each of the four behavioural quadrants represents a state of leadership, not a fixed identity. This distinction is critical when coaching others. You're not labelling people. You're helping them locate a behavioural pattern and giving them the power to shift it.

Anchor behaviours like avoidance, control, or delay are not signs of incompetence; they're signs of safety-seeking. Storm behaviours like reactivity, blame, or domination often mask fear or a lack of emotional regulation. When you frame behaviours this way, it changes how your team receives feedback. It creates psychological safety. You're not saying 'You're the problem,' you're saying 'Let's check this together.'

Use the Shiftcode Quadrants visual during team debriefs or one-to-ones. Ask, 'Which quadrant do you think we were leading from during that project phase?' Let them reflect first, and then coach from there.

Shiftcode Quadrants

Step 2: Use the four codes as coaching levers

Once you've helped someone locate their current quadrant, you now have a framework to help them shift. This is where the Shiftcode Compass becomes your coaching toolkit. Each code offers a behavioural focus area:

- **Awareness:** What patterns am I repeating?

- **Resilience:** How do I stay steady when things go wrong?

- **Authenticity:** Am I leading in a way that aligns with who I really am?

- **Intentionality:** What kind of leader do I want to be, and how will I behave to become that?

These are coaching prompts. When used well, they unlock powerful conversations about behaviour, identity, and leadership development.

For example, you notice a team member constantly overcorrecting their reports after receiving feedback, slipping into perfectionist control. Try asking them:

- When you get feedback, what goes through your mind? (Awareness)

- What do you do next? How does that impact your confidence or energy? (Resilience)

- Are you trying to get it 'right' or trying to grow? (Authenticity)

- What would be a more empowering way to respond to feedback next time? (Intentionality)

This is real-time behavioural coaching, and it's how you help others evolve.

Step 3: Coach the culture, not just the task

Too many leaders coach only in crisis or for correction, but behavioural leadership means coaching even when things are going well, so that positive patterns become embedded.

Celebrate Sail behaviours when you see them (curiosity, composure, agility, and team thinking). Highlight Lighthouse moments (when someone grounded the team, realigned with their values, or communicated with purpose). By naming and reinforcing these behaviours, you send a powerful cultural message: *This is who we are. This is what we do here.*

Daniel Coyle, author of *The Culture Code*, found that high-performing cultures constantly reinforce behavioural norms, not through slogans, but through consistent, emotionally intelligent feedback (2018). Coaching is the delivery system for culture.

Create a team ritual where you reflect monthly on quadrant shifts. Ask:

- Where did we show up as the Sail?
- Where did we feel like we slipped into the Storm?
- What did we learn from that, and what will we do differently next month?

Step 4: Build a coaching synergy

Integration beats intensity. A single powerful feedback session is helpful, but regular and safe behavioural check-ins build long-term transformation.

Here's how to coach using the synergy of the Shiftcode Model:

- Weekly one-to-ones: Use the quadrant language to explore challenges. For example, ask, 'Which quadrant did that reaction come from?'

- Monthly team debriefs: Reflect on quadrant behaviours during projects. Celebrate Sail and Lighthouse moments. Reframe Anchor/Storm slips as learning.

- Quarterly reviews: Align growth plans with the four codes. Create a mini-development plan around the code they need most.

This way, you're guiding behavioural excellence.

Every time you lead from the codes, when you pause to reflect, when you coach instead of command, and when you name the quadrant rather than blame the person, you reinforce a culture of behavioural accountability. Your coaching becomes the ripple effect, your team learns to coach each other, your culture evolves from reactive to conscious, and you no longer carry the weight of leadership alone, because you've multiplied your presence.

The Shiftcode Model is never just about you. It's about who you help others become because of how you choose to lead.

Powerful coaching prompts using the Shiftcode Model

Behavioural coaching requires curiosity, courage, and consistency. When you integrate the Shiftcode Model into your team conversations, you're no longer giving feedback to someone but inviting reflection with someone. You're facilitating insight.

Use these coaching prompts to guide conversations with empathy and precision:

- Which quadrant do you feel you're operating from right now? (This immediately reduces defensiveness. Instead of labelling behaviour as wrong, you help the person locate themselves on the map with curiosity, not criticism.)

- What triggered that response? (This invites emotional awareness. It helps your team members build insight into their default patterns instead of shaming the emotion behind the behaviour.)

- What impact did that behaviour have on the team? (This connects intention to impact, a foundational principle of behavioural leadership.

It helps them see beyond their actions to how those actions shape culture.)

- Which code do you think you could practise to shift into a more effective space? (This reframes the moment from 'you made a mistake' to 'you have a choice'. It builds agency and accountability and you move into coaching for growth.)

Together, these prompts create a psychologically safe environment where feedback becomes fuel and not fire.

Use silence strategically. After asking a coaching question, pause, hold the space, and let them reflect. Insight often lives just beyond the noise.

Team activities and workshops

As well as encouraging self-awareness, the Shiftcode Model creates a shared leadership language. When an entire team uses the same framework, ownership increases, empathy deepens, and culture shifts.

Here are some ideas on how to integrate the model into team development:

- **Quadrant mapping exercise:** This builds vulnerability, depersonalises tension, and encourages mutual support. It turns 'your behaviour' into 'our development'.

- Have each team member privately identify their default quadrant under pressure and the quadrant they aspire to lead from more consistently. Then facilitate a group discussion (voluntary sharing only) about what support they need to make that shift.

- **Behavioural impact dialogue:** This activates empathy and behavioural literacy. People begin to feel the difference, not just understand it intellectually.

- Split into pairs or small groups. Give each group a realistic scenario (eg a tight deadline missed, cross-team conflict, poor feedback delivery). Ask them to first act it out from the Anchor or Storm then replay it from the Sail or Lighthouse. Reflect on how it felt.

- **Code of the month practice:** This makes development ongoing and observable. It keeps behaviour top-of-mind and reinforces learning through repetition.

- Choose one code (eg authenticity) and have the team practise it in real time for two weeks. Encourage daily journaling or pair reflections, then debrief together at the end. Invite team members to share wins, shifts, or struggles.

- For example, Authenticity Month challenge: 'In one meeting this week, practise the 5% truth.' Resilience Month challenge: 'Use AURA in a high-pressure moment and share what changed.'

Creating psychologically safe team discussions

As mentioned in the first chapter, research from Google's Project Aristotle revealed that psychological safety, not compensation, intelligence, or seniority, is the most critical factor in high-performing teams (Duhigg, 2016). Safety is created not through policy, however, but through behavioural leadership.

To create safety using the Shiftcode Model, lead with your own quadrant reflections. For example, 'Last week, I caught myself slipping into Anchor during a meeting. I was hesitant and avoided a direct conversation. I'm working on shifting into Sail.'

Use the codes to invite feedback by asking questions such as: 'What's one way I could show up with more intentionality this month?' or 'How safe do you feel speaking openly on our team right now?' Then respond with presence, not performance. If someone gives you feedback, thank them, even if it stings. Model the self-leadership you're asking for.

Team dialogue prompts could include:

- Where do we, as a team, tend to default to when things get hard?

- Which code would most help us strengthen our collaboration or trust right now?

- What do we need more of and less of to become a Lighthouse team?

When teams have a shared language for patterns, safety, and growth, the culture no longer relies on a hero leader but becomes self-sustaining.

Coaching in the moment and coaching over time

To coach in the moment, use quadrant and code language in real time to shift the energy, interrupt reactivity, or depersonalise tension. For example, 'I sense we're leaning into Storm right now. Let's pause and check what's driving that urgency,' or 'Feels like we're in Anchor. Are we avoiding something we need to face?'

To sustain coaching over time, use one-to-ones and team reflections to support development across the four codes. For example, 'Let's focus on resilience this quarter. What's one trigger you'd like to manage differently?' or 'Over the next two weeks, how will you practise intentionality in your leadership presence?'

These conversations move development from being reactive to being proactive, abstract to embodied, and move personal growth to collective mastery.

You don't need to be a certified coach to coach powerfully. You just need language that builds clarity instead of shame, presence that invites truth instead of silence, and consistency that reinforces the standard you want others to rise to.

Your team aren't watching only your KPIs; they're watching how you behave when the pressure rises and learning how to lead by watching how you lead them.

When you coach with the Shiftcode Model, you're transforming presence and mentoring leaders. Coach wisely, coach boldly, and coach with the Shiftcode Compass in hand.

As you coach your team through behavioural shifts, you're not just developing individual leaders; you're shaping a new standard. Sustainable change isn't solidified in one-to-one conversations or coaching moments alone, though. It's embedded into how things are done every day, how meetings are run, how feedback is given, and how decisions are made.

To make the Shiftcode Model stick, you need to move beyond the personal and into the cultural. That's where we're headed next.

PART FOUR
INTEGRATION INTO WORKPLACE CULTURE

You've done the inner work. You've deepened your awareness, built your resilience, embraced authenticity, and committed to intentionality. You've even started to coach and shift those around you.

Now the real leadership challenge begins. How do you turn a personal practice into a cultural norm? Behavioural excellence isn't sustainable unless it's embedded.

This next part is about collective transformation. It's about scaling the Shiftcode Model into a sustainable, system-wide operating rhythm – a new way of thinking, speaking, relating, and performing.

In this part of the journey, you'll learn how to embed the Shiftcode Model into team rituals, systems, and everyday leadership rhythms, transform behavioural language into a shared standard for how people lead and collaborate, and improve your internal culture so that trust, alignment, and emotional intelligence become organisational trademarks.

This is where the Shiftcode Model becomes the standard. This is where culture is no longer left to chance. This is where you stop reacting and start reshaping the way your organisation shows up in the world.

EIGHT

Rooting Behavioural Intelligence In Culture

L eadership isn't just personal – it's also cultural. The Shiftcode Model doesn't stop with you. It begins with you, but it's meant to extend beyond you.

In the previous chapter, we discussed how to coach and develop others through the Shiftcode Model, moving from personal practice to collective excellence. Coaching individuals alone isn't enough, though. If you want to create a lasting impact, you must lead a cultural shift, and what gets rewarded, repeated, and reinforced in a culture is behaviour.

Culture is defined by how people behave under pressure; it is shaped in the hallway more than in the handbook; and it is felt in feedback conversations, in how meetings are run, in how decisions are made, and in the tone leaders use when things go wrong.

This chapter is about making the Shiftcode Model part of the way you work, not just the way you lead. It's about incorporating behavioural intelligence into your team's language, your organisation's frameworks, and your culture's daily rhythm so that it becomes a new standard, not just a temporary shift.

Culture is a practice, and when you change behaviour, you change everything.

The hidden cost of a toxic culture

Toxic culture is rarely loud at first. It's subtle and usually starts with eye rolls in meetings, sarcasm that goes unaddressed, silence in the face of confusion, or jokes that mask discomfort. Over time, these moments add up. What began as minor dysfunction becomes the norm: people stop speaking up, trust erodes, and psychological safety disappears. With it, creativity, collaboration, and commitment also leave.

According to the 2022 *MIT Sloan Management Review*, toxic culture is ten times more likely to drive attrition than compensation (Sull, 2022). That means people leave not for money but because of how it feels to work in your organisation, and what shapes that feeling is behaviours. The manager who punishes mistakes with public criticism, the executive team that avoids addressing bullying in the name of not rocking the boat, and the silence that follows a brave question.

Toxic culture isn't always caused by malicious intent. More often, it's the by-product of behavioural blind spots that were never addressed and emotional climates that were never stabilised. Unchecked stress, poor communication, unclear accountability, and unspoken resentment take a toll on people's mental health and create environments of chronic tension, psychological exhaustion, and invisible trauma.

People don't heal in the same environment that harmed them. You can't coach your way out of toxicity. You have to shift the culture at the behavioural level.

Gallup's *State of the Global Workplace 2022* report found that employees who are engaged but not thriving in their well-being are at a 61% higher risk of ongoing burnout compared with those who are both engaged and thriving. And research from Boston Consulting Group shows that psychological safety dramatically reduces attrition risk: employees in low-psychological-safety environments face a 12% risk of leaving, compared with just 3% in high-safety environments (Yousif et al, 2024).

Many workplaces, however, still treat well-being as a perk – an app, a wellness Wednesday, or a mental health seminar – rather than addressing the root: how people feel in their day-to-day interactions.

Mental health at work is shaped less by yoga breaks and more by how your manager responds to a mistake, whether you feel heard in meetings, if you're afraid to take leave, whether performance expectations are clear or constantly shifting, and whether you're rewarded for overworking or encouraged to rest.

Culture shapes mental health, and leaders shape culture.

This is why psychological safety is a non-negotiable, especially in a world where uncertainty is the norm, pressure is constant, and emotional resilience is stretched thin. The greatest thing you can offer your people is a safe place to grow, stretch, and speak honestly.

Behaviour at scale and the shadow of leadership

Culture isn't written in your brand guidelines or your corporate values deck. It's written in the tone of your team meetings, the hallway conversations, the tension no one names, and the trust that either expands or contracts based on how leaders behave when things go wrong.

Culture is nothing more than the collective experience of leadership, scaled. Under pressure, what's true comes to the surface. Leaders might intend to build an open, engaged, high-performing culture, but if tension arises, they withdraw, blame, micromanage, or go silent, and that becomes the real culture.

As Harvard's Dr Ronald Heifetz reminds us, leadership is less about titles or speeches and more about helping people face reality and make progress on difficult challenges. His work on *adaptive leadership* underscores that results come not from attributes but from behaviours that mobilise people toward meaningful change. Recent research continues to draw on his insights. For example, Krauter's 2025 article cites *The Practice of Adaptive Leadership* (Heifetz, 2009) as a foundation for rethinking how leaders sustain culture under pressure. Ultimately, culture is what drives sustainable results – and culture is revealed most clearly in how we behave at the pressure points.

Culture is not what you announce but what you allow. The most powerful culture-shaping tool you have is your leadership behaviour.

Every micro-behaviour from leadership becomes a signal: a sigh in a meeting can communicate disapproval, a tone of urgency can stir anxiety, and a pattern of avoidance can suggest that discomfort isn't welcome. In her seminal research, Dr Amy Edmondson (1999) showed that psychological safety is what enables people to take interpersonal risks – speaking up not because it is comfortable, but because the environment makes it safe to be uncomfortable. More than two decades later, reviews of the literature confirm how enduring her insights are: Edmondson and Bransby (2023) found that psychological safety continues to be a cornerstone of learning behaviours, trust, and effective collaboration across industries. Whether in traditional teams or today's virtual workplaces, the evidence is clear – leaders shape the 'learning zone' through the micro-behaviours they model every day.

When leaders demonstrate humility, respond non-defensively to feedback, name their own blind spots, and actively invite challenge, they send a powerful signal: *This is a space where your voice matters. You won't be punished for being human.* That's the beginning of a thriving culture.

The oft-quoted phrase, 'Culture eats strategy for breakfast,' widely attributed to Peter Drucker, reminds us that even the sharpest strategy will falter in the face of a misaligned or toxic culture. While no published record confirms Drucker ever said these exact words, the phrase was already circulating in management circles by 2000. What remains true is the principle: when leaders behave with emotional intelligence and behavioural clarity, teams rise; when they default to silence, micro-management, or emotional volatility, teams shrink.

Leaders often believe that values shape culture. Values are meaningless, however, if they are not mapped to specific, observable behaviours. A plaque on the wall that reads 'Respect' means nothing if interruptions, defensiveness, or passive avoidance dominate meetings. This is why the Shiftcode Compass is so essential. It transforms vague ideals into tangible behaviours.

You don't embed values; you behave them.

In the world of leadership, psychological safety has become the currency of high-performing teams. It's often misunderstood. As Dr Amy C Edmondson explains in *The Fearless Organization: Creating Psychological Safety in the Workplace for Learning, Innovation, and Growth* (2018), psychological safety isn't about niceness; it's about candour. It's the ability to speak up, challenge ideas, admit mistakes, and ask questions without fear of humiliation or punishment.

On the flip side, culture can quietly erode through culture drift: the slow misalignment between what's said and what's done. When behaviours go unchallenged, cynicism sets in. As leaders, the way to interrupt this drift is not with a grand culture programme but with conscious, courageous behaviour.

Why culture matters more than ever

Culture is no longer a soft leadership topic. It's the fuel behind performance, productivity, and progress.

McKinsey & Company reveals that organisations with strong cultures are 3.7 times more likely to be top performers in their industry (2021). Culture is the infrastructure behind every conversation, every decision, and every outcome. A high-performance culture is built on presence.

Now ask yourself the following about your workplace:

- Do people feel psychologically safe to speak up?

- Are behaviours aligned across leaders, departments, and contractors?

- Is feedback delivered with courage and care or fear and fallout?

- Do clients and stakeholders experience consistency, trust, and behavioural intelligence at every touchpoint?

Your internal culture leaks. If it's dysfunctional, fear-driven, or inconsistent, it will shape the way teams interact with customers, suppliers, vendors, and even regulators. Culture is contagious. That's why organisations that embed behavioural intelligence don't just thrive internally but become more competitive, more trustworthy, and more sustainable.

Culture is your internal currency and your external advantage. It's what keeps teams engaged when uncertainty hits, what makes feedback conversations honest rather than harmful, what creates cohesion between departments, contractors, and consultants, and what shapes how clients experience your brand and whether they come back.

When your internal culture is anchored in trust, psychological safety, and clear behaviour expectations, it creates consistency across every touchpoint, from internal stakeholders to external partners, clients, suppliers, and vendors. Your culture becomes your customer experience.

As Simon Sinek writes in *Leaders Eat Last*, 'Customers will never love a company until the employees love it first' (2014). If the people inside your organisation don't feel seen, valued, or safe to contribute, you can guarantee that disconnect will show up in how your teams show up for others.

How people behave inside your organisation is exactly how your organisation behaves externally. It's the tone in an email to a client, the responsiveness of your support team, the way your procurement officer speaks to a supplier, and the difference between a transactional vendor relationship and a trusted partnership.

If your team don't feel safe to speak up internally, they're unlikely to raise potential risks with a client until it's too late. If your leaders operate in a blame culture, you'll see it echoed in vendor escalations, contractor disputes, and fragmented service delivery. If your internal meetings are reactive or emotionally charged, don't be surprised when external partnerships feel tense or erratic.

The reverse is also true and powerful. When your team is grounded in trust, they bring calm to high-pressure client conversations. When collaboration is real, your people partner with suppliers rather than just managing them. When psychological safety is modelled at the top, your people bring curiosity, openness, and professionalism into every negotiation, review, and relationship.

Behavioural clarity in culture makes teams braver, faster, and more unified, not because they're perfect, but because they are safe, clear, and accountable.

This is why culture is not an HR initiative, a branding campaign, or a Friday-morning tea. It's a leadership imperative. When your people feel seen, valued, and clear on how to behave, everyone connected to your business feels it.

Culture is the silent differentiator that wins trust, retains clients, deepens partnerships, and sustains performance. It starts not with posters but with behaviours. Behaviours that are modelled, expected, and embedded every day.

Scaling through practice and not posters

This is where cultural rituals play a role. The following ideas will help create a thriving culture in your workplace:

- Feedback Fridays: where leaders model giving and receiving honest feedback

- Quadrant check-ins: quick moments in team meetings to name behavioural patterns

- Codes of the month: focusing team attention on practising one of the codes with stories, recognition, and micro-practices

When these practices are repeated, they become part of the team. That's where culture starts to shift from being aspirational to being lived.

This behavioural consistency produces a multiplier effect:

- When one person owns a mistake, others do the same.

- When a leader shares a moment of doubt, it creates space for vulnerability.

- When feedback is welcomed with curiosity, trust accelerates.

The returns aren't just cultural but commercial.

Culture is not a side project or a one-off initiative. It is the way your organisation breathes, decides, reacts, and relates every day. And it begins with your next conversation.

Ask yourself:

- What behaviours do I model under pressure?

- What am I normalising through my silence?

- What rituals am I reinforcing through consistency?

- What kind of culture will exist because of me?

Culture is created not just through what you say but through how people feel when you walk into the room.

Embedding the Shiftcode Model

The Shiftcode Model offers a practical, human-centred framework for building behavioural alignment across every level of your organisation, from individual awareness to team dynamics to systemic cultural design.

Embedding the Shiftcode Model into your culture means you're creating the conditions for others to follow, grow, and thrive. You're shifting behaviour at scale. To make this shift real across your organisation, you must move from inspiration to integration. Here's how.

Redesign values as behaviours

Many organisations proudly display their values – 'Integrity. Respect. Innovation' – but values only influence culture when they're translated into observable behaviours.

The Shiftcode Model in action

From vague to visible. Use the four codes to define what each value looks like in practice.

- Integrity with awareness might sound like: 'I notice when my words and actions are out of alignment, and I own it.'

- Respect with resilience might mean: 'I remain composed and respectful even when facing disagreement or pressure.'

When every team member can identify, model, and reflect on the behaviours that bring your values to life, culture becomes lived, not laminated.

Embed the Shiftcode Model into leadership competencies

Leadership capability frameworks often focus on achieving outcomes, managing resources, hitting targets, and making decisions, but few address how those outcomes are achieved behaviourally.

The Shiftcode Model in action

- Integrate the Shiftcode Quadrants and the Shiftcode Compass into leadership assessments, 360 reviews, and capability frameworks.

- Evaluate not just what was achieved but how through feedback, collaboration, emotional regulation, and presence under pressure.

- Use behavioural journaling and coaching conversations to reflect on quadrant patterns and personal development.

This elevates leadership from performance-focused to presence-focused, reinforcing that how leaders behave matters just as much as what they deliver.

Build shared language across teams

The most cohesive cultures speak a shared behavioural language. They can name what's happening without blame because they've normalised the conversation around energy, emotion, and patterns.

The Shiftcode Model in action

- Introduce the Shiftcode Quadrants in team onboarding and training sessions.

- Create 'quadrant check-ins' in team meetings: 'Where are we showing up from right now?'

- Use codes of the month for behavioural focus: 'This month, we're practising resilience; what's one way we're modelling that?'

When teams have shared language, they develop shared accountability. Peer-to-peer coaching becomes easier, feedback becomes less personal, and behavioural shifts become a team standard, not a personal struggle.

Make behaviour a strategic KPI

Culture is often considered intangible, but the truth is that it's deeply measurable when you know what to look for.

The Shiftcode Model in action

- Track behavioural metrics in engagement surveys. Include questions like 'I feel safe to speak up on my team', 'My leader models behaviour that aligns with our values', and 'We constructively address tension'.

- Review quadrant patterns across departments and identify coaching needs.

- Link behavioural excellence to career progression and recognition, not just technical achievement.

When you measure behaviour with the same seriousness as revenue, culture becomes part of your competitive edge.

The Shiftcode Model is a developmental blueprint that shows you what's possible. It turns vague values into vivid behaviours, transforms emotional reactivity into emotional maturity, and creates a culture that endures.

Touchpoint reflection

How is your internal behaviour showing up externally? This reflection is your opportunity to pause, zoom out, and assess the alignment between your internal culture and the way your organisation is perceived, experienced, and trusted in the world.

In his book, *Leadership BS*, Stanford professor Jeffrey Pfeffer argues that culture is revealed less by what leaders say than by how they behave in the hard moments – especially when no one is watching (2015). Behaviour is the most reliable measure of culture, and it is contagious. Recent studies affirm this: leaders' resilient behaviours spread to their teams, fostering resilience in others (Caniëls and Curşeu, 2024); and negative behaviours like rudeness quickly ripple through workplaces when they go unchecked (Borders and Jacobson, 2024). In other words, what leaders model under pressure doesn't just reveal culture – it multiplies it.

Use the prompts below to reflect. They're not here to judge your culture but to see it clearly.

Team to client

According to Gallup's *2020 Q12 Meta-Analysis*, work units with higher employee engagement show significantly better customer loyalty and perceptions, comparing favourably across diverse industries (Harter et al). As we've discussed, if your team is frustrated or unsupported, those feelings inevitably shape the customer (or client) experience.

- How do your team members speak about client issues when the client isn't in the room?

- When mistakes happen, is the default response defensiveness, blame, or transparency?

- Do clients experience your people as present, calm, and solution-oriented or as reactive and avoidant?

Leader to contractor

Ambiguity, sarcasm, or emotional outbursts damage working relationships. Contractors talk, and they influence your brand reputation, whether you realise it or not.

- How do your leaders behave under pressure in meetings with contractors or consultants?

- Is feedback delivered with respect and clarity or emotional volatility and control?

- Are relationships built on partnership or hierarchy and compliance?

Internal culture to customer experience

According to Forrester's *Global Total Experience Score Rankings, 2025*, companies that align their brand promise with the experiences they deliver outperform competitors – achieving up to 3.5x revenue growth, along with significantly higher customer retention and loyalty. When your people feel seen, safe, and supported, they deliver the same experience outwards.

- Does your frontline team feel empowered to solve problems, or do they fear repercussions?

- Are service issues handled with empathy or with policy-driven rigidity?

- Would your customers describe your team as engaged, confident, and consistent or as transactional and unpredictable?

Procurement to supplier

Long-term vendor success is built on trust. Supply chain resilience, especially post-pandemic, depends on strong relationships.

- Are suppliers treated as valued partners or as replaceable vendors?

- Is your communication proactive and collaborative or reactive and transactional?

- Do suppliers feel safe to raise challenges or pressured to stay silent?

Now take a moment to reflect on these simple and powerful questions:

- What is one internal behavioural habit at the leadership, team, or cultural level, that may be silently impacting how your organisation shows up to the outside world?

- What's one behaviour you're willing to shift to build greater trust across every touchpoint?

Your next behavioural shift could transform your entire value chain. That's not just leadership but legacy in motion.

Embedding behavioural intelligence in culture is a continuous, lived experience. It's what transforms teams from compliant to committed, from fractured to unified, and from transactional to inspired. Embedding is only the beginning.

What does leadership look like when behavioural intelligence is not just a practice but a presence? How do we lead when the world keeps changing faster than our titles can adapt?

In the final chapter, we look beyond the frameworks. We discuss the new face of leadership excellence – one that's agile, emotionally grounded, and systemically aware. The future doesn't need more traditional leaders; it needs transformed ones, and that future begins with how you choose to lead next.

NINE

The New Face Of Leadership Excellence

W ell done – we've now reached the last chapter of this book. This is not the end but the beginning of a new way of leading. We are stepping into a new leadership era that's shaped not by hierarchy or titles but by humanity.

Gone are the days when authority alone commanded loyalty or when charisma could substitute for character. In a world filled with volatility, complexity, and continuous transformation, teams need presence.

Your team is watching how you show up when a meeting turns tense and how you steady the room when stress levels rise. They are paying attention to what your presence feels like, especially when the pressure hits.

This is what the future demands: not performative leadership but behavioural excellence.

Redefining success in leadership today

True leadership is no longer defined by how many people report to you or how much power your title implies. It's defined by how much safety, space, and strength you create for others. It's about the energy you bring into the room, not the noise you make while you're in it.

In this era, leadership success is measured by your ability to elevate. Do people find their voice in your presence? Do they take more ownership because of how you lead – not in fear, but in trust? Do they leave interactions with you feeling clearer, braver, and more aligned with their potential?

That's the shift. It's about being a quiet force of confidence and clarity, asking the questions that unlock new thinking, and making space for others to shine.

Leadership in this era is about presence and permission. It's about grounding your impact in values that outlast the project or the pay cheque. As Marshall Goldsmith reminds us in his work on leadership legacy, the true test of leadership is not what happens while you are in the room, but what continues after you are gone. That is legacy.

Success today is influence, and influence is not about controlling people but about earning trust and shaping belief. Real success is defined by the clarity you model, especially when things get messy, uncertain, or emotionally charged.

Success is measured in the ripple effect of your behaviour. This is the leadership shift you've been building throughout this book:

- From leading for output to leading for impact

- From operating in silos to shaping systems of behavioural excellence

- From performance-driven personas to people-driven presence

- From having the answers to asking more powerful, perspective-shifting questions

The new leadership standard isn't about getting more done but about helping people become more who they're meant to be because of how you lead them. You are no longer just accountable for hitting milestones. You're responsible for the emotional and psychological climate you create in meetings, on calls, and in how you respond when pressure hits.

As Maya Angelou once wrote, 'I've learned that people will forget what you said, people will forget what you did, but people will never forget how you made them feel' (1993). This is the new leadership standard;

not dictated from above but lived from within – not about being in charge, but about behaving appropriately when others are watching, and especially when they're not.

It begins with the same question the Shiftcode Model has asked you from the start: who are you choosing to be in the moments that matter most?

Excellence as a collective outcome

The most powerful cultures are built in the unnoticed moments: in the space between back-to-back meetings, in the way leaders respond when someone fumbles, in who's encouraged to speak and who's interrupted, in the tone of an email, and in the pause before a difficult truth is spoken or buried. This is where culture lives: not in slogans but in signals.

The most sustainable, inspiring cultures are shaped when excellence becomes a shared behavioural commitment. When people at every level choose to raise the standard because someone modelled how – this is when culture stops being aspirational and becomes operational.

A thriving culture isn't a trickle-down effect. It's an inside-out phenomenon that starts with one person choosing to show up differently and spreads as others see what's possible when values are lived, not just spoken.

The most contagious force in an organisation isn't energy or optimism but integrity in action. Behavioural integrity, which is the alignment between what we say and what we do, isn't something you can demand. It's something people feel and follow.

Let's make it real:

- When your feedback invites reflection, not defence, you're showing your team how to be honest and curious at the same time.

- When your resilience anchors the room, you become the steady presence by which others can orient themselves.

- When you lead with unpolished, honest authenticity, you let others stop performing and start connecting.

- When your intentionality sets the tone, you lift the energy in a way that helps others show up with purpose – not to impress, but to create real impact.

This is how the shift scales from individual change to collective cultural momentum.

You don't create a high-performing team by commanding excellence. You create it by modelling it visibly, imperfectly, and consistently. In doing so, you invite a powerful new standard: one where excellence is not a title but a habit.

This is how culture begins to rewrite itself.

People call themselves forward not to avoid blame but to own impact. They catch one another in the act of leading well, not just in the wins, but in the way they handle the setbacks. They don't wait for the right environment; they start creating it.

That's when culture stops being a leader's burden and becomes everyone's opportunity. That's the DNA of leadership excellence – where the expectation is not perfection but practice, where performance is not driven by pressure but powered by people, and where the win is not just delivering results but doing it in a way that uplifts others.

It begins, always, with how you show up and whether you stay long enough in the discomfort to let the shift become who you are, not just what you do.

Sustaining the shift: Staying in the practice

You've come this far – you've decoded patterns, reflected deeply, and mapped out a different way of leading – but this book is the beginning. The Shiftcode Model isn't something you finish but something you embody.

Transformation lives in how you respond when the stakes are high, and the script disappears. It's in the tension you walk into tomorrow, the silence you hold when emotions rise, the courage you summon to name the thing no one else will, the grace you extend when someone misses the mark.

In those moments, you have a choice: autopilot or awareness, habit or reflection, image or integrity, comfort or clarity. Those choices, repeated often enough, build trust, culture, and legacy.

To be clear, you will get it wrong sometimes. That's not failure – it's feedback. What matters is how you recover. As James Clear writes in *Atomic Habits*, 'Every action you take is a vote for the type of person you wish to become' (2018). In leadership, every behaviour you choose is a vote for the culture you wish to create.

Stay in the practice. Don't wait for a title, a new strategy, or a company-wide initiative. Just start where you are. The missed deadline, the tense team call, and the stressed-out colleague aren't distractions from your leadership. They are the curriculum. They are the moments that matter.

Choose:

- Awareness over assumption
- Resilience over reaction
- Authenticity over perfection
- Intentionality over inconsistency

Do it again, and again, and again. Culture doesn't shift when you read the book. It shifts when you live the book. You don't need more leadership theory. You need real-time tools, support, and opportunities for accountability that hold you to the leader you've chosen to become.

The shift isn't over. It's just beginning, and it starts with you.

Conclusion

You've reached a threshold. The moment when insight meets choice, when understanding invites action, and when your leadership shifts from something you do to someone you are.

Throughout this journey, you've paused to reflect on patterns. You've uncovered the cost of unconscious behaviours: how silence can erode trust, how emotional volatility can suppress engagement, how control can block collaboration, and how misalignment can dim inspiration.

More importantly, you've seen what's possible when you lead from a different place. When you steady yourself in awareness, you disrupt autopilot. When you practise resilience, you hold steady in uncertainty. When you embody authenticity, you create safety through realness. When you lead with intentionality, you move others with purpose and clarity.

These are behavioural codes that create a lasting impact within you, around you, and beyond you. Your legacy won't be defined by how many reports you filed, how many projects you completed, or how many targets you hit. It will be defined by how people feel in your presence. By how deeply they trusted you, how you made them feel seen, safe, and significant, and how you showed up when the moment required character, which is more than competence.

That's the shift. What now?

You've done the reflective work, mapped your quadrant, explored the four codes, and witnessed the power of the Shiftcode Model in your leadership journey. Transformation isn't sustained in silence, though. It's strengthened in the community. It's scaled through shared language, and it's reinforced when you choose to keep going – together.

If you're ready to take this further and embed this shift into your daily behaviour, your team dynamic, and your organisational culture, then I invite you to join me in the Shiftcode Leadership Excellence Accelerator Program: www.empoweredbydesign. com.au/organisations.

It's where behavioural mastery becomes muscle memory, reflection becomes real-time recalibration, and leaders don't just understand the model but become it. If you're ready to move from inspiration to implementation, from insight to integration, and from a good leader to a transformational presence... join us.

This isn't a course or another leadership training. It's a behavioural transformation experience where committed leaders come together to practise excellence.

In this space, you will be:

- Mentored through real-world application of the Shiftcode Model

- Held accountable to the behaviours you want to build

- Challenged to rise above reactivity and lean into conscious leadership

- Equipped with the tools, language, and frameworks to shift culture from the inside out

This is your next level. Your opportunity to turn insight into integration, to go from knowing the shift to living it. Leadership excellence is about choosing to realign and not faltering.

Your culture and team are not looking for perfect leaders. They're looking for present ones, consistent ones, and human ones. They're looking for someone willing to do the work continuously. That's the power of behavioural leadership, the essence of the Shiftcode Model, and the legacy you're capable of creating.

The shift begins now, and it starts with you.

Let's lead on purpose together.

References

Angelou, M (1993). *Conversations with Maya Angelou* (J. M. Elliot, Ed.). University Press of Mississippi.

Baldoni, J (2019). *Grace: A leader's guide to a better us*. Indigo River Publishing.

Bandura, A (1986). *Social Foundations of Thought and Action: A Social Cognitive Theory*. Prentice-Hall.

Basford, T, and Schaninger, B (11 April 2016). 'The four building blocks of change'. McKinsey & Company. www.mckinsey.com/capabilities/people-and-organizational-performance/our-insights/the-four-building-blocks--of-change, accessed 5 September 2025.

Bennis, W (2009). *On Becoming a Leader*. Basic Books.

Borders, M, and Jacobson, R (20 June 2024). 'New research shows that workplace rudeness is "contagious"'. University of New

Mexico Anderson School of Management. https://business. unm.edu/news/highlights/2024/06/new-research-shows-tha t-workplace-rudeness-is-contagious.html, accessed 22 September 2025.

Brassey, J, De Smet, A, Kothari, A, Lavoie, J, Mugayar-Baldocchi, M, and Zolley, S (2 August 2021). 'Future proof: Solving the "adaptability paradox" for the long term'. McKinsey & Company. www.mckinsey.com/capabilities/people-an d-organizational-performance/our-insights/future-proo f-solving-the-adaptability-paradox-for-the-long-term, accessed 5 September 2025.

Bresman, H, and Edmondson, AC (17 March 2022). 'Research: To excel, diverse teams need psychological safety'. *Harvard Business Review*. https://hbr.org/2022/03/research-to-excel-divers e-teams-need-psychological-safety, accessed 5 September 2025.

Brim, B (9 March 2021). 'Successful leadership: The 4 needs of followers'. Gallup. www.gallup.com/cliftonstrengths/ en/334373/successful-leadership-4-needs-followers.aspx, accessed 5 September 2025.

Brown, B (2018). *Dare to Lead: Brave work. Tough conversations. Whole hearts*. Random House.

Brown, B (15 October 2018). 'Clear is kind. Unclear is unkind'. https://brenebrown.com/articles/2018/10/15/clear-i s-kind-unclear-is-unkind, accessed 22 September 2025.

Brown, B (1 May 2019). 'Let's rumble'. https://brenebrown.com/ articles/2019/05/01/lets-rumble, accessed 22 September 2025.

Buckingham, M, and Coffman, C (1999). *First, Break All the Rules: What the world's greatest managers do differently*. Simon & Schuster.

Camp, A, Gast, A, Goldstein, D, and Weddle, B (12 February 2024). 'Organizational health is (still) the key to long-term performance'. McKinsey & Company. www.mckinsey.

com/capabilities/people-and-organizational-performance/
our-insights/organizational-health-is-still-the-key-to-long-te
rm-performance, accessed 5 September 2025.

Caniëls, CJ, and Curşeu, P (2024). 'Contagious resilience –
how leaders' resilient behaviour promotes followers' resilient
behaviour'. *Leadership & Organization Development Journal*, 45(5),
754–770. www.emerald.com/lodj/article/45/5/754/1218110,
accessed 22 September 2025.

Charan, R, and Conaty, B (2010). *The Talent Masters: Why smart
leaders put people before numbers*. Crown Business.

Clear, J (1 June 2021). 'Identity-based habits: how to actually stick
to your goals this year'. James Clear. https://jamesclear.com/
identity-based-habits, accessed 5 September 2025.

Clear, J (2018). *Atomic Habits: An easy & proven way to build good
habits & break bad ones*. Avery.

Clifton, J, and Vigers, B (11 February 2025). 'What do
people need most from leaders?' Gallup. www.gallup.com/
workplace/655817/people-need-leaders.aspx, accessed
5 September 2025.

Collins, J (2001). *Good to Great: Why some companies make the leap…
and others don't*. Harper Business.

Corporate Leadership Council (2004). 'Driving performance and
retention through employee engagement: Executive summary'.
Corporate Executive Board.

Covey, SR (2012). *The Wisdom and Teachings of Stephen R. Covey*.
Simon & Schuster.

Cox, J (25 April 2025). 'Poor Workforce Engagement Cost
World Economy $438 Billion in 2024'. *Forbes*. www.forbes.com/
sites/josiecox/2025/04/25/poor-workforce-engagement-cos
t-world-economy-438-billion-in-2024, accessed 22 September 2025.

Coyle, D (2018). *The Culture Code: The secrets of highly successful groups*. Bantam Books. Retrieved from https://youexec.com/book-summaries/the-culture-code-by-daniel-coyle, accessed 5 September 2025.

D'Auria, G, Nielsen, NC, and Zolley, S (2020). 'Tuning in, turning outward: Cultivating compassionate leadership in a crisis'. McKinsey & Company. www.mckinsey.com/capabilities/people-and-organizational-performance/our-insights/tuning-in-turning-outward-cultivating-compassionate-leadership-in-a-crisis, accessed 22 September 2025.

David, S (2016). *Emotional Agility: Get unstuck, embrace change, and thrive in work and life*. Avery.

De Smet, A, Dowling, B, Hancock, B, and Schaninger, B (13 July 2022). *The Great Attrition is making hiring harder. Are you searching the right talent pools?* McKinsey & Company. www.mckinsey.com/capabilities/people-and-organizational-performance/our-insights/the-great-attrition-is-making-hiring-harder-are-you-searching-the-right-talent-pools, accessed 5 September 2025.

Deloitte (2023). '2023 Human Capital Trends'. Deloitte Insights. www.deloitte.com/us/en/insights/topics/talent/human-capital-trends/2023.html, accessed 23 September 2025.

DiLeonardo, A, Phelps, RL, and Weddle, B (27 July 2020). 'Establish a performance culture as your "secret sauce"'. McKinsey & Company. www.mckinsey.com/capabilities/people-and-organizational-performance/our-insights/the-organization-blog/establish-a-performance-culture-as-your-secret-sauce, accessed 23 September 2025.

Dispenza, J (2008). *Evolve your brain: The science of changing your mind*. Health Communications.

Duhigg, C (28 February 2016). 'What Google learned from its quest to build the perfect team'. *The New York Times*. www.

nytimes.com/2016/02/28/magazine/what-google-learned-fro
m-its-quest-to-build-the-perfect-team.html, accessed
5 September 2025.

Dweck, CS (2006). *Mindset: The new psychology of success*. Random
House.

Edelman (2022). '2022 Edelman Trust Barometer: The cycle
of distrust'. www.edelman.com/trust/2022-trust-barometer,
accessed 5 September 2025.

Edelman (2022). '2022 Edelman Trust Barometer Special Report:
Trust in the workplace. www.edelman.com/trust/2022-trust-
barometer/special-report-trust-workplace, accessed 5 September
2025.

Edmondson, AC (1999). 'Psychological safety and learning
behavior in work teams'. *Administrative Science Quarterly*,
44(2), 350–383. https://journals.sagepub.com/doi/
abs/10.2307/2666999, accessed 5 September 2025.

Edmondson, AC (2018). *The Fearless Organization: Creating
Psychological Safety in the Workplace for Learning, Innovation, and
Growth*. John Wiley & Sons.

Edmondson, AC, and Bransby, D (2023). 'Psychological
safety comes of age: Observed themes in an established
literature'. *Annual Review of Organizational Psychology and
Organizational Behavior*, 10, 91–117. https://doi.org/10.1146/
annurev-orgpsych-120920-055217.

Eurich, T (19 October 2018). 'Working with people who aren't
self-aware'. *Harvard Business Review*. https://hbr.org/2018/10/
working-with-people-who-arent-self-aware, accessed 23
September 2025.

Eurich, T (2017). *Insight: Why we're not as self-aware as we think,
and how seeing ourselves clearly helps us succeed at work and in life*.
Crown Business.

Feiner, M (2004). *The Feiner Points of Leadership: The 50 basic laws that will make people want to perform better for you*. Warner Business Books.

Forrester (24 June 2025). 'Global total experience score rankings, 2025'. Forrester Research. www.forrester.com/press-newsroom/forrester-total-experience-score-2025-rankings, accessed 23 September 2025.

Frankl, VE (1946). *Man's Search for Meaning*. Beacon Press.

Gallup (2021). *State of the Global Workplace*: 2021 Report. Gallup, Inc. www.visualcapitalist.com/wp-content/uploads/2021/06/state-of-the-global-workplace-2021-download.pdf, accessed 24 September 2025.

Gallup (2022). *State of the Global Workplace*: 2022 Report. Gallup, Inc. https://millennium-challenge.com/wp-content/uploads/2023/01/state-of-the-globa l-workplace-2022-download-1.pdf, accessed 24 September 2025.

Gallup (2023). *State of the Global Workplace*: 2023 Report. Gallup, Inc. https://advisor.visualcapitalist.com/wp-content/uploads/2023/06/state-of-the-global-workplace-2023-download.pdf, accessed 24 September 2025.

Gallup (2024). *State of the Global Workplace*: 2024 Report. Gallup, Inc. https://elements.visualcapitalist.com/wp-content/uploads/2024/08/state-of-the-global-workplace-2024-download.pdf, accessed 24 September 2025.

Gallup (2025). *State of the Global Workplace*: 2025 Report. Gallup, Inc. https://healthyworkcompany.com/wp-content/uploads/2025/05/state-of-the-global-workplace-2025-download.pdf, accessed 24 September 2025.

Gallup (no date). 'Leadership'. www.gallup.com/topic/category-leadership.aspx, accessed 5 September 2025.

Gallup (no date). 'Leadership'. www.gallup.com/topic/category-leadership.aspx, accessed 5 September 2025.

George, B, and Sims, P (2007). *True North: Discover your authentic leadership*. Jossey-Bass.

George, B, Sims, P, McLean, AN, and Mayer, D (2007). 'Discovering your authentic leadership'. *Harvard Business Review*, 85(2), 129–138. https://hbr.org/2007/02/discovering-you r-authentic-leadership, accessed 5 September 2025.

Goldsmith, M (2007). *What Got You Here Won't Get You There: How successful people become even more successful*. Hyperion.

Goleman, D (1995). *Emotional Intelligence: Why it can matter more than IQ*. Bantam Books.

Goleman, D (1998). *Working with emotional intelligence*. Bantam Books.

Goleman, D (2000). 'Leadership that gets results'. *Harvard Business Review*, 78(2), 78–90. https://hbr.org/2000/03/leadership-that-gets-results, accessed 5 September 2025.

Goleman, D (2004). 'What makes a leader?' *Harvard Business Review*, 82(1), 82–91. https://hbr.org/2004/01/what-makes-a-leader, accessed 5 September 2025.

Goleman, D (2006). *Social intelligence: The new science of human relationships*. Bantam Books.

Goleman, D (2013). 'The focused leader'. *Harvard Business Review*, 91(12), 50–60. https://hbr.org/2013/12/the-focused-leader, accessed 5 September 2025.

Goleman, D, Boyatzis, R, and McKee, A (2002). *Primal leadership: Unleashing the power of emotional intelligence*. Harvard Business School Press.

Gottman, JM (2012). *What makes love last?: How to build trust and avoid betrayal*. Simon & Schuster.

Grant, A (2013). *Give and Take: Why helping others drives our success*. Viking.

Guggenberger, P, Maor, D, Park, M, and Simon, P (26 April 2023). 'The State of Organizations 2023: Ten shifts transforming organizations'. McKinsey & Company. www.mckinsey.com/capabilities/people-and-organizational-performance/our-insights/the-state-of-organizations-2023, accessed 23 September 2025.

Harter, J et al (October 2020). 'The relationship between engagement at work and organizational outcomes — 2020 Q12® meta-analysis (10th ed.)'. Gallup. https://media-01.imu.nl/storage/happyholics.com/6345/gallup-2020-q12-meta-analysis.pdf, accessed 23 September 2025.

Heath, C, and Heath, D (2010). *Switch: How to change things when change is hard*. Broadway Books.

Heifetz, RA, Grashow, A, and Linsky, M (2009). *The practice of adaptive leadership: Tools and tactics for changing your organization and the world*. Harvard Business Press.

HRO Today (2025). 'Workplace Values Misaligned with Leadership Behavior'. www.hrotoday.com/company-culture/workplace-values-misaligned-with-leadership-behavior, accessed 23 September 2025.

Kaplan, S (2017). *The Invisible Advantage: How to create a culture of innovation*. Greenleaf Book Group Press.

Kaufman, SB (6 November 2019). 'Can empathetic concern actually increase political polarization?' Beautiful Minds. https://blogs.scientificamerican.com/beautiful-minds/can-empathic-concern-actually-increase-political-polarization/, accessed 5 September 2025.

Kegan, R, and Lahey, LL (2013). *Immunity to change: How to overcome it and unlock the potential in yourself and your organization*. Harvard Business Press.

Kissinger, H (2022). *Leadership: Six studies in world strategy*. Penguin Press.

Kong, F (2023). *Leadership Excellence: Passion, purpose, productivity, & perspective*. National Book Store.

Korn Ferry Institute (17 November 2013). *A better return on self-awareness*. www.kornferry.com/insights/briefings-magazine/issue-17/better-return-self-awareness, accessed 23 September 2025.

Kotter, JP (1996). *Leading change*. Harvard Business School Press.

Kotter, JP, and Rathgeber, H (2006). *Our Iceberg Is Melting: Changing and succeeding under any conditions*. St. Martin's Press.

Kouzes, JM, and Posner, BZ (2003). *Encouraging the Heart: A leader's guide to rewarding and recognising others*. Jossey-Bass.

Kouzes, JM, and Posner, BZ (2011). *The Five Practices of Exemplary Leadership* (2nd ed). John Wiley & Sons.

Krauter, J (2025). 'Re-Envisioning Leadership Practice for an Uncertain Future: A Conceptual Synthesis Based on Critical Realist View and Quantum Principles'. *Open Journal of Leadership*, 14(1), 1-54. https://doi.org/10.4236/ojl.2025.141001

Lacerenza, CN, Reyes, DL, Marlow, SL, Joseph, DL, and Salas, E (2017). 'Leadership training design, delivery, and implementation: A meta-analysis'. *Journal of Applied Psychology*, 102(12), 1686–1718. https://doi.org/10.1037/apl0000241.

Lencioni, P (2002). *The Five Dysfunctions of a Team: A leadership fable*. Jossey-Bass.

Maxwell, JC (2007). *The 21 Irrefutable Laws of Leadership: Follow them and people will follow you*. Thomas Nelson.

Maxwell, JC (2011). *The 5 Levels of Leadership: Proven steps to maximize your potential*. Center Street.

McKinsey & Company (10 September 2024). 'What is leadership: A definition and way forward'. www.mckinsey.com/featured-insights/mckinsey-explainers/what-is-leadership, accessed 5 September 2025.

Mirkhan, SD, Omer, SK, Ali, HM, Hamza, MY, Rashid, TA, and Nedunchezhian, P (2 May 2024). 'Effective Delegation and Leadership in Software Management'. arXiv. https://arxiv.org/abs/2405.01612, accessed 5 September 2025.

Nadella, S (2017). *Hit Refresh: The quest to rediscover Microsoft's soul and imagine a better future for everyone.* Harper Business.

Omadeke, J (22 July 2022). 'The best leaders aren't afraid to be vulnerable'. *Harvard Business Review.* https://hbr.org/2022/07/the-best-leaders-arent-afraid-of-being-vulnerable, accessed 23 September 2025.

Pfeffer, J (2015). *Leadership BS: Fixing workplaces and careers one truth at a time.* Harper Business.

Robin, C, and Bradford, DL (2004). *Leadership Excellence and the 'Soft' Skills: Authenticity, Influence, Performance.* Stanford Graduate School of Business. www.gsb.stanford.edu/faculty-research/working-papers/leadership-excellenc e-soft-skills-authenticity-influence-performance, accessed 5 September 2025.

Rossman, J (2014). *The Amazon Way: 14 leadership principles behind the world's most disruptive company.* Clyde Hill Publishing.

Schein, EH (2017). *Organisational culture and leadership* (5th edition). Wiley.

Society for Human Resource Management (2024). 'The State of Global Workplace Culture in 2024'. SHRM. www.shrm.org/topics-tools/research/the-state-of-global-workplace-cultur e-in-2024, accessed 22 October 2025.

Siegel, DJ, and Bryson, TP (2011). *The whole-brain child: 12 revolutionary strategies to nurture your child's developing mind.* Delacorte Press.

Sinek, S (2009). *Start with Why: How great leaders inspire everyone to take action.* Portfolio.

Sinek, S (2014). *Leaders Eat Last: Why some teams pull together and others don't*. Portfolio.

Skinner, BF (1953). *Science and human behavior*. Macmillan.

Sternfels, B, Pacthod, D, Strovink, K, and Howard, W (22 October 2024). 'The art of 21st-century leadership: From succession planning to building a leadership factory'. McKinsey & Company. www.mckinsey.com/capabilities/strategy-and-corporate-finance/our-insights/the-art-of-21st-cent ury-leadership-from-succession-planning-to-building-a-leader ship-factory, accessed 5 September 2025.

Sull, D, Sull, C, and Zweig, B (11 January 2022). 'Toxic Culture Is Driving the Great Resignation'. *MIT Sloan Management Review*, 63(2), 1–9. https://sloanreview.mit.edu/article/toxic-cultur e-is-driving-the-great-resignation, accessed 23 September 2025.

Sun Tzu (2005). *The Art of War* (L. Giles, Trans.). El Paso Norte Press. (Original work published ca. 5th century BCE).

TalentSmart (2009). *The business case for emotional intelligence*. TalentSmart.

Terry, RW (1993). *Authentic Leadership: Courage in action*. Jossey-Bass.

Tracy, B (2012). *12 Disciplines of Leadership Excellence: How leaders achieve sustainable high performance*. AMACOM.

van Dam, N, and van der Helm, E (1 February 2016). 'The organizational cost of insufficient sleep'. McKinsey & Company. www.mckinsey.com/capabilities/people-an d-organizational-performance/our-insights/the-organizationa l-cost-of-insufficient-sleep, accessed 5 September 2025.

Williams, P, and Denney, J (2018). *Leadership Excellence: The seven sides of leadership for the 21st century*. Advantage Media Group.

Wooden, J, and Jamison, S (2005). *Wooden on Leadership: How to create a winning organization*. McGraw-Hill.

Xiang, N (12 December 2024). 'SHRM report: Workplace Culture Fosters Employee Retention Worldwide'. *SHRM*. www.shrm. org/executive-network/insights/shrm-report-workplace-cultur e-fosters-employee-retention, accessed 5 September 2025.

Xu, H, et al (2023). *The Impact of Heterogeneous Shared Leadership in Scientific Teams*. arXiv. https://arxiv.org/abs/2306.15804, accessed 5 September 2025.

Yousif, N, Dartnell, A, May, G, and Knarr, E (4 January 2024). 'Psychological safety levels the playing field for employees'. Boston Consulting Group. www.bcg.com/publications/2024/ psychological-safety-levels-playing-field-for-employees, accessed 22 September 2025.

Zak, PJ (2017). 'The Neuroscience of Trust'. *Harvard Business Review*, 95(1), 84–90. https://hbr.org/2017/01/ the-neuroscience-of-trust, accessed 23 September 2025.

Zenger, J, and Folkman, J (2024). *From Boomers to Millennials: The unexpected strengths of each generation's leaders*. Zenger Folkman.

Acknowledgements

This book exists because of the countless people who have shaped my understanding of what it means to lead with intention, presence, and heart.

To my late parents, who taught me resilience, integrity, and the power of unwavering belief. Your love and wisdom laid the foundation for everything I have become. Your teachings live on in every page.

To my son, Ekhraj, who has been my greatest teacher, who shows me daily that true leadership begins with authenticity and heart. You made it easy for me, as a single mum, to navigate the challenges I faced. You never made demands, never complained. Your grace and understanding gave me strength.

To my niece, Jasmine, who represents the next generation of strong female leaders and reminds me why this work matters.

To my friends, colleagues, mentors, and fellow leaders who walked alongside me – thank you for your courage to challenge, your honesty to reflect, and your willingness to support me in the moments that mattered most. The people around us shape the leader within us, and your presence has been a mirror, a compass, and a steady foundation in my journey.

To every leader willing to look in the mirror, shift their behaviours, and choose excellence over comfort.

This is for you, with deep gratitude and appreciation.

The Author

Preetie Boler hasn't just studied leadership – she's lived it, mastered it, and transformed it.

A facilitator, mentor and speaker, Preetie specialises in behavioural leadership, transforming how organisations develop their leaders and create thriving teams and workplace cultures. A former construction lawyer with thirty years of legal and commercial leadership experience, Preetie led high-stakes negotiations, resolved complex disputes, and learned one powerful truth: behaviours drive results. With this unique background, she brings a deep understanding of high-stakes environments and complex organisational dynamics.

She is the creator of the innovative Shiftcode Model, a behavioural framework designed to close the gap between potential and performance by addressing the behavioural blind spots that quietly undermine leadership effectiveness. Her work is born from decades of experience in legal, construction, and corporate settings, where she witnessed firsthand how leadership behaviours – not just technical skills – drive team performance and cultivate thriving workplace cultures.

Her obsession with transforming behaviours led her to become a certified emotional intelligence facilitator and mindfulness practitioner. Preetie's human-centred approach empowers leaders to shift from reactive patterns to cultivating behavioural intelligence for intentional leadership that builds trust, fosters engagement, drives collaboration and inspires excellence – the four pillars every modern workplace needs.

Preetie's methodology is practical, immediately applicable, and tailored to the real-world challenges of today's leadership. Through facilitating workshops and mentorship programs using the frameworks, she helps leaders unlock new levels of performance, foster genuine engagement, and build a legacy of excellence.

⊕ www.empoweredbydesign.com.au

in www.linkedin.com/in/preetie-boler

www.ingramcontent.com/pod-product-compliance
Lightning Source LLC
Chambersburg PA
CBHW070349200326
41518CB00012B/2187